# COUNTRY COOKING

# COUNTRY COOKING

ED. SUZANNE SMITH

© 2011 Kerswell Farm Ltd

This edition published by King Books

Printed 2011

This book is distributed in the UK by
Parkham Books Ltd
Barns Farm, Boraston
Tenbury Wells
Worcestershire
WR15 8NB

david@kingbooks.co.uk

ISBN: 978-1-906239-74-9

DS0211. Country Cooking

Creative Director: Sarah King
Project editor: Anna Southgate
Designer (internal): Paul Stewart-Reed
Photographer: Colin Bowling/Paul Forrester

Material from this book previously appeared in *Allotment Cookbook, 100 great recipes - Chinese, Healthy Eating - best ever recipes, Diabetic - best ever recipes, Farmers market - best ever recipes, 100 great recipes - Indian, Meals in minutes - best ever recipes, 100 great recipes - Pasta, Potato - best ever recipes, 100 great recipes - Vegetarian.*

Printed in China

1 3 5 7 9 10 8 6 4 2

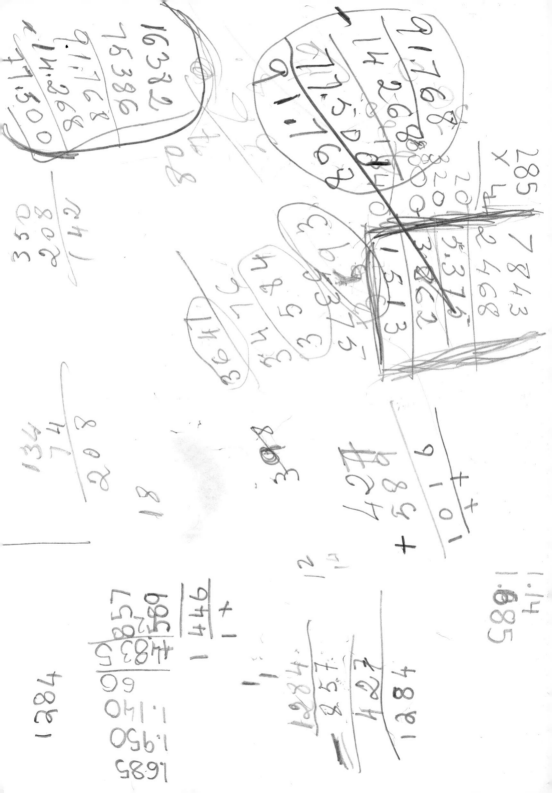

# Contents

| | |
|---|---|
| Introduction | 6 |
| Picnic Time | 14 |
| With Friends | 36 |
| Quick Prep - Slow Cook | 58 |
| Feeling Thrifty | 82 |
| Healthy Eating | 106 |
| Exciting Recipes for Children | 132 |
| Straight from the Veg Patch | 154 |
| Particularly Delicious | 178 |
| Yummy Treats | 200 |
| Index | 222 |

# introduction

It is only in relatively recent years that we have been able to enter a supermarket and choose from a vast range of ready-made meals. All we have to do on returning home after an exhausting day is to remove a cardboard sleeve, pierce a plastic film and open a bottle of wine. Dinner can be over and done with in a matter of minutes. But is this a good thing? Can we call it progress? Depending on how often we do the above, it might not be. Certainly, there is a degree of progress, as it can be a relief to know that, sometimes, there is no need to plan a meal, but that we can simply make a selection. From time to time, this can be of benefit to everyone. But convenience food, I fear, has morphed from an occasional option to a staple of our weekly shopping. Of course, there is a place in the Western diet for convenience food, but it should not dominate our lives. Hopefully, this book will help to bring back the enjoyment and pleasure of simple traditional cooking, with both contemporary and traditional recipes. Above all, it should demonstrate that, when the time is right, basic cooking can be almost as quick, almost always as economical and always tastier and healthier than the pre-packed option.

When it comes to food, you are living in world of incredible choice, where there are many options for you to choose from in shops and eateries, whether buying a sandwich at a service station or deciding on a menu for entertaining or looking to fulfill a sudden craving with a treat. In each chapter of this book, the aim is to cover most food eventualities that you come across in such situations in a bid to encourage you to revert back to the alternative of preparing and cooking your own food from scratch.

Although the title of this book is Country Cooking, don't let this put you off if you live in a high-rise flat in the middle of a well-populated city. Try thinking of the title as an expression of the country that you live in and what is available to you right here on every doorstep and changing from season to season.

You may want to convert yourself completely from a convenience food calamity to a confident home cook. This will require a bit of rethinking from most angles, but can be done painlessly with just a bit of planning. Use the chapters in this book to start your mind and imagination

flowing. Think about the kinds of food you buy on a weekly and daily basis, and why? Do your choices revolve around time, convenience, taste or money? Whatever your reasons, there are plenty of alternatives to be found in this book. Plan what you need to stock yourself for the week ahead and make a shopping list so that it doesn't become a chore. Once your habits and attitude towards food have evolved you will be able to enjoy the spontaneity of cooking wholesome, tasty food from scratch. This book is packed full of delicious and scrummy recipes that suit all walks of life and different occasions. It shows that good home cooking can be easy, quick and above all very satisfying.

## Something new?

Not everyone has the ability to visit a farmers' market on a regular basis, but many now operate at the weekend and are a fantastic way to find exactly the right type of seasonal, local and fresh produce, linking directly to country cooking. You may not be able to get everything on your shopping list from your local farmers' market. All I ask is that you buy at least some of your food there. Your reward is that you will begin to discover the joy of buying good-quality, seasonal ingredients on a regular basis. You will also learn that shopping for food can be both informative and fun.

### What is a farmers' market?

A farmers' market is a, usually fortnightly, event at which you can buy food produced by local farmers, growers and producers. They come from a defined area and sell direct to the public. All the products available are grown, reared, caught, brewed, pickled, baked, smoked or processed by the stallholders. There will always be staples such as fruit and vegetables, salads, cheeses, meat, poultry, breads and eggs. But farmers markets also sell speciality foodstuffs such as honey, juices, preserves, wine, cider, milk, cream, cakes, fish and herbs. The produce is seasonal, so the stalls in a farmers market will vary throughout the year, with the greatest choice in the summer and rather less in winter. However, you can expect to find unusual varieties and produce that you do not find in the supermarkets, such as quinces, sloes, golden beetroot, as well as unpasteurised milk and cream. A true farmers market will have no commercial stalls or stalls selling items that have not been produced locally.

Some products at farmers markets are not available all year round, especially fruit and vegetables. However, farmers are putting up more polytunnels and hothouses each year, thereby extending the seasons of many of our fruits and vegetables. Nevertheless, the farmer still has to rely on sun and rain, so supply will vary.

## REALLY USEFUL TIPS

### Buying vegetables

**Root vegetables**
- Avoid too much dirt on vegetables, but do expect them to be dirty. Supermarket vegetables are always cleaned.
- Make sure the vegetables are firm and not shrivelled.
- Avoid large swedes that may have woody centres.
- If buying bunched carrots, the tops should look fresh.

**Green vegetables**
- Choose vegetables with a bright and strong colour.
- Avoid those with yellow-tinged leaves.
- Store wrapped in paper bags or newspaper.

**Salad vegetables**
- Select fresh looking leaves.
- Cucumbers should be firm.
- Salad onions should have fresh unshrivelled leaves.

### Buying fruit:

**Apples and pears**
- Avoid fruit with bruises.

**Summer fruit**
- Avoid very soft fruits with any signs of mushiness.
- Choose strawberries with good all-over colour, avoiding those with unripened white flesh around the stem.

## Educate yourself

You may like to begin to educate yourself on where your meat, poultry, fish and game have come from. Even general supermarket butchers are far more savvy on the origins and general welfare of meat they sell, so when purchasing meat, ask about the breed and animal welfare. Where possible, buy native breeds. If you are lucky enough to have suppliers of rare breeds, do not be put off by the term feeling that because they are rare, you should not be eating them. Instead, consider them more as traditional breeds that need the demand of the consumer to ensure their survival. Just as varieties of fruit taste different, so breeds of animals have their own unique characteristics and flavours. Many of the rare-breed meats became so because they did not suit modern, more intensive methods of production – they mature more slowly and usually on a natural diet. As a result, their meat is of a higher quality. I urge you to try these traditional breeds. In doing so, you are ensuring their survival and will be in for a truly great taste experience.

## Cut out the middlemen

In no time at all you may have re-thought your weekly shop, where you do it, what you buy, how you cook and certainly what you are eating. You may even decide to have a go at growing your own fruit and vegetables.

You may never have grown even a single lettuce before, but it really isn't difficult to turn a small patch of ground into a thriving allotment and there is never a better time to start than the present.

If you are a gardener, you will find growing and harvesting your own produce very satisfying. Whether you have a small or a large garden, a plot of land or an allotment, you will reap the fruits of both spring and summer planting, but may find that many of them are in abundance at the same time. From high summer onwards you will be gathering in crops at their peak of ripeness.

The pleasure of gathering in the harvest to make jams, jellies and chutneys is timeless and universal. Furthermore, homemade preserves make beautiful gifts for friends and family.

So take a break from the garden and turn your kitchen into a hive of activity. Indulge in baking and making delicious meals. Fill your freezer to the brim and your pantry with pots of perfect preserves full of colour and texture from the fruits and vegetables you have so lovingly grown in your garden.

# Tips for Preserving

Preserving is one of the oldest forms of cooking and, for many years, cooks have enjoyed preparing summer fruits and vegetables and preserving them for use throughout the cold days of winter. This is a satisfying activity and many cooks enjoy it as a leisure pastime with a sense of nostalgia for the old-fashioned ways of generations before them.

• Herbs should be picked on a dry day, before flowering. Snip off any large stalks and discard any damaged leaves from the herb. Plunge into a bowl of cold water and swish around to remove any grit or dirt. Arrange the herbs in small bunches and tie each with a piece of string. Hang upside down to dry in full sunshine, bringing the bunches indoors a tnight to protect from evening moisture. After 3 to 4 days the herbs should be completely dried. If you cannot dry the herbs in sunshine, place them on a wire rack in a cool oven or anairing cupboard.

• When the leaves crumble easily the herbs are ready to store. Untie the bunches and rub the leaves off the stalks and store in dry jars or airtight tins in a dry, dark place. Mint, basil, thyme, parsley, oregano, rosemary and bay leaves all dry very successfully in bunches int his way.

• Most vegetables can be frozen, with the exception of salad vegetables like lettuce ,cucumber and whole tomatoes. For best results choose young vegetables that have just reached their peak before freezing.

•Vegetables need to be blanched before freezing to destroy the enzymes present in them that will otherwise cause them to deteriorate. Blanching also helps retain the colour, texture and flavour of vegetables.

# Blanching vegetables

Prepare vegetables as you would for cooking by trimming into neat pieces or slicing thinly.

Bring 4l/7pt water to the boil with 2 tsp salt for every 450g/1lb of vegetables. Add the vegetables in a basket if possible, and return to the boil for one minute after the vegetables are added.

Remove the vegetables with a slotted spoon and plunge into a large bowl of iced, cold water to cool the vegetables as quickly as possible. Use new cold water for each batch.

Drain and toss the vegetables to separate them. For large pieces such as broccoli or cauliflower, spread on a clean tea towel to dry. Pack into plastic bags or boxes, label and freeze immediately.

# Picnic Time

A picnic can vary enormously in style. It could be a grand formal event where everyone sits at a table, with place mats, a tablecloth, pretty napkins, tasteful crockery and even candelabras. But more often than not a picnic is a convenient way to eat outside on a rug on a warm sunny day. Whichever you choose,there are very few other more pleasant ways to share time and food with family and friends. Here are a collection of recipes that can be used or adapted for either occasion.

# Rustic Pie

This colourful pie tastes good at any time of year. Serve it hot or at room temperature.

**Ingredients for 4-6**

100g/4oz wholemeal flour
100g/4oz plain flour
100g/4oz butter or margarine, diced
250g/9oz small new potatoes
2 tbsp olive oil
1 red onion, peeled and thinly sliced
2 red peppers, deseeded and thinly sliced
100g/4oz feta cheese, crumbled
salt and freshly ground black pepper
1 beaten egg

1 Place the flours in a bowl and add margarine or butter. Rub the fat into the flour with your fingertips until the mixture resembles rough breadcrumbs. Stir in 4 tbsp cold water with a knife. Use your hands to form the mixture into a dough. Chill for at least 30 minutes in fridge.

2 Place the potatoes in a pan of boiling water and cook for 10 minutes until tender. Drain and cut into quarters when cooled.

3 Heat the oil in a large frying pan and cook the onion and pepper over a moderate heat for 5–8 minutes, stirring from time to time until softened.

Remove from the heat and stir in the potatoes. Cool.

4 Remove the pastry from the fridge. On a lightly floured surface roll the pastry out in a rough circle to a thickness of 6mm/¼in. Place on a lightly oiled baking sheet.

5 Add the feta cheese, along with salt and pepper to taste, to the potato and peppers. Pile this mixture into the middle of the pastry. Brush the edges with beaten egg. Roughly draw up the edges, pinching together to form an edge. Bake in the preheated oven for 30 minutes. Serve.

# Smoked Salmon & Cucumber Pasta Salad

I like to serve this dish in the summer as it is ideal for alfresco eating. You can use smoked salmon trimmings for this salad, which are much cheaper than sliced smoked salmon. For a tasty variation use "hot smoked" trout.

## Ingredients for 2

150g/5oz pasta
50g/2oz smoked salmon
1/4 cucumber
1 tsp chopped fresh dill
3 tbsp soured cream
Grated zest 1/4 lemon
Salt and freshly ground
    black pepper
Fresh dill sprigs to garnish

## Ingredients for 4

275g/10oz pasta
100g/4oz smoked salmon
1/2 cucumber
2 tsp chopped fresh dill
100ml/31/2fl oz soured cream
Grated zest 1/2 lemon
Salt and freshly ground
    black pepper
Fresh dill sprigs to garnish

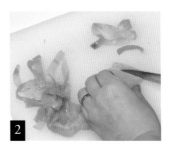

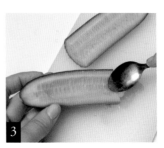

1 Cook the pasta in plenty of lightly salted boiling water for 10 minutes or as directed on the packet. Drain and cool under cold running water, drain again and place in a mixing bowl.

2 Cut the smoked salmon into slivers and add to the pasta.

3 Cut the cucumber in half lengthways and scoop out the seeds.

4 Cut the cucumber in half again lengthways then thickly slice and add to the pasta.

5 Combine the dill, soured cream and lemon zest. Season lightly.

6 Pour the soured cream dressing over the pasta and toss to combine.

7 Transfer to a serving dish and garnish with fresh dill.

# Carrot & Pea Flan

A lovely veggie flan that's completely dairy free.

## ingredients for 4-6

175g/6oz wholewheat flour
175g/6oz self-raising flour
175g/6oz dairy-free
   vegetable margarine
Cold water
900g/2lb carrots
1 red onion
1 clove garlic
4 tbsp olive oil

50g/2oz fresh/defrosted
   frozen peas
4 tsp chopped parsley (fresh
   or dried)
150ml/¼pt soya milk
4 eggs
Salt and pepper

1 To make pastry, sift the flours and salt into a mixing bowl, adding any grains left in the sieve. Cut margarine into small cubes and add to flour. Use your fingertips lightly to rub the fat into the flour to make "breadcrumbs".

2 When the mixture looks crumbly sprinkle about 2tbsp of water over the mixture and use your hands to mix ingredients into smooth dough. Add more water as needed.

3 The bowl should be clean and no bits of flour left behind. Wrap the pastry in plastic wrap and rest it in the fridge for 30 minutes. Roll out on a floured surface and use to line a 22cm/9in pie tin.

4 Peel carrots and grate. Peel onion and chop. Peel garlic and crush.

5 Heat oil in a frying pan and cook grated carrots, chopped onion and crushed garlic gently for 10 minutes with a lid on the pan. Stir in peas and chopped parsley. Put pan to one side to cool.

6 Evenly arrange mixture in the pastry case. Measure milk in a jug, add eggs and seasoning and pour over filling. Then place in a preheated oven (200°C/400°F/Gas 6) for 25–30 minutes.

# Spicy Beef and Potato Crescents

These pastry bites are great for parties. I have given the quantity for a smaller amount but they can be frozen uncooked and thawed when required.

## Ingredients for 2

**1 tbsp olive oil**
**½ small onion, chopped**
**1 clove garlic, chopped**
**½ chilli, seeded and chopped**
**100g/4oz potato, peeled and diced**
**75g/3oz lean mince beef**
**¼ tsp each cumin, coriander and turmeric**
**75ml/2½fl oz water**
**225g/8oz shortcrust pastry**
**beaten egg to glaze**

## Ingredients for 4

**2 tbsp olive oil**
**1 small onion, chopped**
**2 cloves garlic, chopped**
**1 chilli, seeded and chopped**
**200g/7oz potato, peeled and diced**
**175g/6oz lean mince beef**
**½ tsp each cumin, coriander and turmeric**
**150ml/¼pt water**
**450g/1lb shortcrust pastry**
**beaten egg to glaze**

1 Heat the oil in a frying pan and sauté the onion and garlic for 3–4 minutes until softened.

2 Add the chilli and potato and sauté for 5 minutes, turning frequently.

3 Add the meat and cook until browned, breaking up with a spoon as it cooks. Add the spices and water.

4 Simmer for 20 minutes until the potato is tender and the liquid has evaporated.

5 Roll the pastry on a lightly floured work surface and cut out 7.5cm/3in circles.

6 Pile a little of the meat filling into each centre. Fold over the pastry and pinch edges together to seal. Repeat until all the pastry and filling is used.

7 Brush with beaten egg. Bake in a preheated oven 200°C/400°F/gas mark 6 for 15–20 minutes until golden.

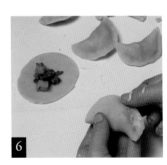

# Chicken Goujons

These are a kid's favourte served with a tomato dip.

Ingredients for 2

8oz/225g chicken breast
1oz/25g plain flour
1 egg
3oz/75g fresh breadcrumbs
Oil for frying

Ingredients for 4

1lb/450g chicken breast
2oz/50g plain flour
2 eggs
4½oz/125g fresh
   breadcrumbs
Oil for frying

1 Cut the chicken breast into long thin strips. Put the flour into a plastic foodbag and add the chicken strips.

2 Hold the bag firmly and shake until all the chicken is evenly coated with flour.

3 Using tongs remove the chicken from the bag; shake off the excess flour as you take the chicken out.

4 Beat the eggs in a bowl and put the breadcrumbs into a plastic food bag.

5 Using tongs, dip a few strips of the chicken into the egg and then add to the bag of breadcrumbs. Shake to cover chicken with crumbs. Put the chicken onto a plate and repeat the process with remaining chicken. Put the chicken in the fridge to chill for 30minutes.

6 Heat 1cm (½in) oil in a frying pan until hot. Add chicken and fry for 5 minutes or until golden brown and cooked through,turning the chicken often.

# Crispy Potato Balls with Chilli Dip

I serve these spicy potato balls with a ready-made sweet chilli dipping sauce, but you could also serve them with a cucumber and yoghurt dip or mango chutney.

## Ingredients for 2

150g/5oz floury potatoes, peeled
75g/3oz carrots, peeled
Salt
50g/2oz frozen peas, thawed
1/2 red chilli, seeded and finely chopped
2 tbsp chopped fresh coriander
2 tbsp gram (chick-pea) flour
A little beaten egg
Oil for deep-frying
Sweet chilli sauce to serve

## Ingredients for 4

300g/10½oz floury potatoes, peeled
150g/5oz carrots, peeled
Salt
100g/4oz frozen peas, thawed
1 red chilli, seeded and finely chopped
4 tbsp chopped fresh coriander
4 tbsp gram (chick-pea) flour
A little beaten egg
Oil for deep-frying
Sweet chilli sauce to serve

1 Cut the potatoes and carrots into 2cm/¾in pieces. Bring a pan of water to the boil. Add a little salt and the potatoes and carrots and cook for 10 minutes until soft. Drain well.

2 Place in a bowl with the peas, chilli and coriander and mash well. Add the gram flour and enough egg to bind.

3 With damp hands shape the potato into small balls. Set aside.

4 Heat the oil for deep-frying to 180°C/350°F. Deep-fry the balls in batches until crisp and golden. Drain on kitchen paper and keep warm until all the balls are cooked.

5 Serve the potato balls with the chilli sauce for dipping.

# Home-made Lemonade

This is a refreshingly tangy summer drink.

**Ingredients**
5 lemons
100g/4oz sugar
1l/1¾pt sparkling water
Ice cubes

Makes: 1 litre /1¾ pt

1 Cut four lemons in half and squeeze thejuice. Pour into large jug.

2 Add sugar and sparkling water, stir well.

3 Slice the remaining lemon. Cut each slice inhalf and add to jug along with approximately10 ice cubes. Serve in drinking glasses.

# Lavender Cookies

A very sophisticated touch to the humble cookie.

## Ingredients for 24 cookies:

125g/5oz caster sugar
1 tbsp lavender flower buds
110g/4½oz unsalted butter, softened
1 tsp vanilla extract
150g/6oz plain flour
¼ tsp bicarbonate of soda

1 Preheat the oven to 190°C (375°F/Gas 5).Grease and line two baking sheets with greaseproof paper.

2 The day before you need the cookies, make the lavender sugar. Place the sugar and flowerbuds in a food processor and whiz for a couple of minutes to break up the lavender flowers. Place in an airtight container and leave overnight for the flavours to infuse.

3 Pass the sugar through a sieve to remove any of the lavender flowers. In a bowl, cream 110g (4oz) of the sugar and the butter together until pale and fluffy. Add the vanilla essence and mix well. Sift in the flour and bicarbonate of soda and stir until well mixed.

4 Wrap the dough in clingflim and leave to chill in the fridge for an hour. On a lightly floured surface, roll the mixture out to ½ cm (¼in) thickness and cut into shapes and transfer to the baking trays. Sprinkle the cookies with the remaining sugar and bake for 10 minutes or until lightly golden. Transfer to a wire rack to cool.

# Lemon Drizzle Cupcakes

Zesty and scrumptious picnic treats.

## Ingredients

110g/4½oz unsalted butter, softened
110g/4½oz caster sugar
2 eggs, beaten
110g/4½oz self-raising flour
Finely grated zest of 1 lemon

### Drizzle topping

125g/5oz granulated sugar
60ml/2fl oz lemon juice

1 Preheat the oven to 180°C (350°F/Gas 4), then line a 12-hole bun tin with paper cases.

2 Cream the butter and sugar together until pale and creamy. Gradually beat in the eggs, a little at a time, beating well after each addition. Fold in the flour and lemon zest, using a metal spoon. If the mixture is stiff, add a couple of spoonfuls of milk for a better dropping consistency.

3 Spoon this mixture into the prepared cases and bake for 15–20 minutes until well risen and golden. Remove from the oven and transfer to a wire rack. Whilst the cakes are still hot, prepare the drizzle topping. Mix the sugar and lemon juice together, but do not let the sugar dissolve.

4 Prick the top of the hot cupcakes with a fork. Pour the lemon drizzle over the still hot cupcakes. The juice will sink into the sponge, leaving a crunchy sugar topping.

# Cherry Cheesecake Slices

These cherry cheesecake slices make the ideal dessert for a picnic, or make a tray of them ahead of time and serve them after a barbecue.

## Ingredients for 12 slices

175g/6oz digestive biscuits
75g/3oz butter, melted
25g/1oz golden granulated
   sugar

### Topping

400g/14oz jar pitted morello
   cherries
2 tsp arrowroot

### Filling

350g/12oz full-fat cream
   cheese
100g/4oz natural caster
   sugar
2 eggs, beaten
½ tsp vanilla essence
2 tsp lemon juice

1 Preheat the oven to 180°C/350°F/Gas 4. Grease and line the base of an 18x27cm/7x11in oblong tin with non-stick baking paper. Place the biscuits in a strong plastic food bag and crush into crumbs by tapping with a rolling pin.

2 Melt the butter in a heavy-based pan and mix in the biscuit crumbs and the granulated sugar. Stir together, then spoon into the tin and spread over the base evenly.

3 Soften the cream cheese together with the caster sugar, then beat in the eggs, essence and lemon juice until smooth. Pour over the biscuit base in the tin. Bake for about 30 minutes until the filling is risen, firm and golden. Cool in the tin, then chill. When cold, remove from the tin and peel away the papers.

4 To make the cherry topping, dissolve the arrowroot powder with 2 tbsp of juice from the cherries. Place the cherries and remaining juice in a heavy-based pan and heat until the juices thicken. Spoon the cherry mixture over the baked base.

5 Leave to cool and set, then cut into 12 slices with a sharp knife.

# With Friends

While some meals you might serve when entertaining require some attention, the last thing you want to be doing when having friends over for is to be spending most of your time in the kitchen. Far nicer to put the thought and effort in beforehand, leaving you more time to enjoy the company. Whether you're serving dinner, lunch, or simply a snack, the trick is minimum fuss with maximum enjoyment.

# Baba Ghanoush

A creamy, smoky, spiced dip that can be served with crudités or spread on toast.

| ingredients for 2 | ingredients for 4 |
|---|---|
| 1 small aubergine | 1 large aubergine |
| 2 tbsp tahini | 4 tbsp tahini |
| 1 tbsp lemon juice | 2 tbsp lemon juice |
| 1 small clove garlic, peeled and crushed | 1 clove garlic, peeled and crushed |
| ½ tsp ground cumin | 1 tsp ground cumin |
| ¼tsp chilli powder | ½tsp chilli powder |
| 1 tbsp fresh coriander, chopped, plus extra for garnish | 2 tbsp fresh coriander, chopped, plus extra for garnish |
| salt and freshly ground black pepper | salt and freshly ground black pepper |
| 1 small rustic loaf | 1 large rustic loaf |

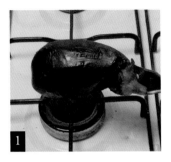

1 Using a large fork or similar implement, spear the aubergine firmly. You need to do this so that you can then slowly roast it over a gas flame until the aubergine becomes soft, tender and shrivelled and the skin is blackened. This will take a few minutes. It can be baked in the oven but it does not give the same flavour.

2 Leave the aubergine until cool enough to handle. Use your fingers to peel away all the skin and discard. You may need to rinse the aubergine quickly under the tap to remove any last scraps of charred skin.

3 Place the aubergine flesh in a sieve and squeeze it to remove as much of the liquid from it as possible. Discard this liquid.

4 Now place the aubergine in a food processor, or blender, with the tahini, lemon juice, garlic, cumin and chilli powder and process until smooth. Spoon the mixture into a bowl and stir through the chopped coriander. Season to taste.

5 Thickly slice the loaf and toast both sides. Serve the baba ghanoush spooned onto the toast, garnished with a little more coriander.

# Mozzarella & Peppers in a Crusty Roll

The combination of crusty bread with creamy mozzarella and roasted peppers makes a perfect lunch or supper. Serve this dish as it is or with a light salad. Note that the peppers could be prepared in advance to the end of step 2 and then reheated when you are ready to eat.

## ingredients for 2

3 large, sweet peppers
1 tbsp olive oil
/2 clove garlic, peeled and
   crushed
½ tsp paprika
60g/2½oz mozzarella cheese
2 large, crusty rolls
Basil leaves to garnish
Salt and freshly ground
   black pepper

## ingredients for 4

6 large, sweet peppers
2 tbsp olive oil
1 clove garlic, peeled and
   crushed
1 tsp paprika
150g/5oz mozzarella cheese
4 large, crusty rolls
Basil leaves to garnish
Salt and freshly ground
   black pepper

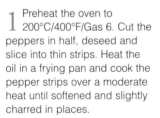

1 Preheat the oven to 200°C/400°F/Gas 6. Cut the peppers in half, deseed and slice into thin strips. Heat the oil in a frying pan and cook the pepper strips over a moderate heat until softened and slightly charred in places.

2 Add the garlic and sprinkle over the paprika, stirring well to mix. Continue to cook over a gentle heat for a further 5 minutes.

3 Drain the mozzarella and pat dry with kitchen paper. Slice thinly and set to one side.

4 Split the rolls in half and divide the peppers between them. Top with slices of mozzarella and cook in the preheated oven for 10 minutes, or until the cheese is melted and golden in places. Garnish with basil leaves and season to taste. Serve.

# Duck & Honey Stir-fry

Oriental flavours combine in this quickly cooked dish that makes an ideal main course for a supper party.

## Ingredients for 2

2 duck breasts
1 tbsp clear honey
2 tbsp soy sauce
1 tsp sesame oil
2 carrots
4 spring onions
½ head Chinese leaf
1 tbsp sunflower oil

## Ingredients for 4

4 duck breasts
2 tbsp clear honey
4 tbsp soy sauce
2 tsp sesame oil
4 carrots
8 spring onions
1 small head Chinese leaf
2 tbsp sunflower oil

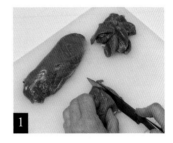

1 Slice the duck breasts thinly and place in a bowl. Mix the honey, soy sauce and sesame oil together, add to the bowl and chill for 5–10 minutes.

2 Cut the carrots into fine matchsticks. Slice the onions and the Chinese leaf thinly.

3 Heat the oil in a wok or a large frying pan. Drain the duck strips and stir-fry for 3 minutes until browned. Remove to a plate and keep warm.

4 Add the sliced vegetables and stir-fry for 4 minutes. Return the duck to the pan with the marinade and stir-fry for a further 2 minutes until hot. Serve with boiled egg noodles.

# Salmon Steaks with Lemon Butter

Lemon and fresh basil provide a delicious fresh topping for salmon steaks and also help to keep the fish moist during baking.

## Ingredients for 2

2 x 150g/5oz salmon steaks
Salt
White pepper
½ lemon
25g/1oz butter, softened
1 tbsp fresh basil, chopped
½ tbsp fresh parsley,
    chopped

## Ingredients for 4

4 x 150g/5oz salmon steaks
Salt
White pepper
1 lemon
50g/2oz butter, softened
2 tbsp fresh basil, chopped
1 tbsp fresh parsley,
    chopped

1 Preheat the oven to 200°C/400°F/Gas 6. Season the fish with salt and white pepper and place in a single layer in a greased ovenproof dish.

2 Grate the zest finely from the lemon and beat into the butter with the chopped herbs.

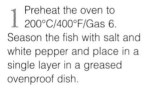

3 Spread the butter over each salmon steak. Cover with foil and and bake for 15 minutes until the fish is tender.

4 Place the salmon on warmed serving plates and spoon over the melted butter from the dish. Serve with new potatoes and steamed mangetout or asparagus tips.

# Beef Pot-roast

A mixture of main crop and sweet potatoes stretch the meat so that a little goes a long way in this super one-pot meal. Even if you are cooking the smaller quantity, you may have some meat left over but do not worry, it is delicious served cold.

## Ingredients for 2

400g/14oz rolled brisket
1 tbsp sunflower oil
100g/4oz shallots, peeled
225g/8oz sweet potato,
    peeled and cut into
    large chunks
175g/6oz main crop
    potatoes, peeled and cut
    into large chunks
200ml/7fl oz beef stock
2 cloves garlic, peeled
Salt and freshly ground
    black pepper

## Ingredients for 4

700g/1½lb rolled brisket
2 tbsp sunflower oil
225g/8oz shallots, peeled
450g/1lb sweet potato,
    peeled and cut into
    large chunks
350g/12oz main crop
    potatoes, peeled and
    cut into large chunks
300ml/½pt beef stock
6 cloves garlic, peeled
Salt and freshly ground
    black pepper

1 Preheat the oven to 180°C/350°F/Gas 4.

2 Season the meat with salt and pepper.

3 Heat the oil in a flameproof casserole and brown the meat quickly on all sides.

4 Add all the remaining ingredients. Cover and cook in the oven for 1½–2 hours depending on the size of the meat.

5 Transfer the meat and vegetables to a serving plate and serve the gravy separately in a jug.

# Pork Tenderloin Roast

A tasty low-fat roast – perfect for Sunday lunch.

## Ingredients for 2

1 small pork tenderloin
½ tsp olive oil
1½ tbsp fresh rosemary,
    chopped
1½ tbsp fresh parsley,
    chopped
½ tbsp black peppercorns
1 tbsp crème fraîche

## Ingredients for 4

1 large or 2 small pork
    tenderloins
1 tsp olive oil
3 tbsp fresh rosemary,
    chopped
3 tbsp fresh parsley,
    chopped
1 tbsp black peppercorns
2 tbsp crème fraîche

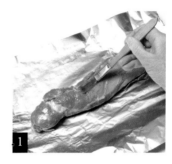

1 Preheat the oven to 375°F/190°C/Gas 5. Brush a large sheet of tin foil with a little of the oil. Place the tenderloin in the centre of the foil. Using the remaining oil, brush the tenderloin all over.

2 In a bowl, mix together the chopped rosemary and parsley. Use a pestle and mortar to roughly crush the peppercorns and add them to the chopped herbs. Mix.

3 Press the herb and pepper mixture over the tenderloin to cover evenly. Pull the tin foil up over the meat to cover loosely and pinch the edges together to seal it. Place in a roasting tin and cook in the preheated oven for 20 minutes per 450g/1lb plus 20 minutes.

4 Once the meat is cooked, remove it from the oven and leave in a warm place for 15 minutes for the meat to rest. At the end of this time, open the foil and pour any juices that have collected into a small saucepan. Stir in the crème fraîche and gently heat to almost boiling. Remove from the heat. Carve the meat into thin slices and serve with the crème fraîche sauce, vegetables and new potatoes.

# Goulash

If you can only find regular paprika, that's fine, but if you can track down some sweet paprika for this dish, it will taste even better (and many supermarkets and delicatessens now stock a far wider range of herbs and spices than they did in the past). I do not recommend using hot paprika, however!

## Ingredients for 2

1 tbsp sunflower oil
1 large onion, peeled and chopped
2 large red peppers, deseeded and chopped
250g/9oz potatoes, peeled and cut into chunks
1½ tbsp paprika
150ml/¼pt vegetable stock
1 x 200g/7oz can cannellini beans, rinsed and drained
Salt and freshly ground black pepper

## Ingredients for 4

2 tbsp sunflower oil
2 large onions, peeled and chopped
4 large red peppers, deseeded and chopped
500g/1lb 1oz potatoes, peeled and cut into chunks
3 tbsp paprika
300ml/½pt vegetable stock
1 x 400g/14oz can cannellini beans, rinsed and drained
Salt and freshly ground black pepper

1 Heat the oil in a large frying pan and cook the onions over a moderate heat until they are tender and softened.

2 Add the chopped peppers and continue to cook for a further 10 minutes, stirring from time to time, until the peppers are soft and starting to turn golden in places.

3 Toss the chopped potatoes in the paprika to coat. Add them to the pan and cook, stirring for 2–3 minutes.

4 Stir in the stock and beans and bring gently to the boil. Now reduce the heat to a gentle simmer.

5 Cook. stirring from time to time, for 40 minutes until the mixture is thickened and the potatoes are tender and starting to break up a little.

6 Season to taste and serve with noodles and sour cream.

# Pinwheel Cookies

Keep this dough stored in the freezer until you are ready to bake it – fresh cookies on demand!

1 Put each set of ingredients in separate bowls. Bring the ingredients together and form a soft dough with a little water. Wrap in clingfilm and freeze for 15 minutes.

2 Roll each dough to a rectangle of about 18 x 25cm (7 x 10in). Brush the mocha dough with a little water, then lie the vanilla dough on top.

3 Roll both doughs together - a little like a swiss roll. Wrap in clingfilm and refrigerate for 30 minutes.

4 Preheat the oven to 180°C (350°F/Gas 4. Grease 2 baking trays. Slice the dough into 18 even slices, about 6cm (¼in) wide. Place on the trays, well-spaced.

5 Bake for 15–20 mintes until firm and lighlty golden. Allow to cool on the trays for 2 minntes, then transfer to a wire rack.

6 Pour this mixture over the base. Bake for a further 5 minutes. Leave to cool in the tin and then cut into slices.

# Cherry Clafouti

An impressive-looking dessert that is very easy to make.

*ingredients for 4-6*

2 x 425g/15oz cans of cherries in juice, drained thoroughly
50g/2oz plain flour
100g/4oz caster sugar
15g/½oz butter, melted
200ml/7fl oz semi-skimmed milk
1 tsp vanilla essence
4 eggs, beaten
Icing sugar for dusting

1 Preheat the oven to 375°F/190°C/Gas 5. Lightly oil a shallow oven-proof dish and scatter the cherries over the base.

2 Sift the flour into a mixing bowl and add the sugar. Stir to mix, then make a well in the centre.

3 Beat the melted butter, milk, vanilla essence and eggs together. Pour this mixture into the flour and sugar and stir until it is smooth and all the flour has been incorporated.

4 Pour the batter over the cherries and bake in the preheated oven for 40 minutes until risen and golden. Allow to stand for 5 minutes. Dust with a little icing sugar before serving.

# Dundee Cake

This long-keeping cake is ideal to make ahead for a special family tea, or as a guess-the-weight cake for a raffle. I think it also makes a great New Year's present.

### Ingredients for 8

400g/14oz mixed dried fruit
50g/2oz ground almonds
150g/5oz butter
150g/5oz golden caster
   sugar

Finely grated zest of 1 lemon
3 eggs, beaten
100g/4oz plain flour
50g/2oz whole almonds,
   skinned

1 Preheat the oven to 180°C/350°F/Gas 4. Grease and line the base and sides of an 18cm/7 inch round, deep cake tin.

2 Place the dried fruits in a bowl with the ground almonds and toss the fruit to coat it evenly.

3 Beat the butter and sugar and lemon zest together until light and fluffy. Whisk in the eggs, a little at a time, adding a teaspoon of flour with each addition.

4 Sift the remaining flour into the bowl and add the dried fruit. Fold together with 1 tablespoon of cold water until smooth and even.

5 Spoon the mixture into the tin, make a slight hollow in the centre, then smooth level. Arrange the almonds over the surface in circles.

6 Bake for 1 hour, then reduce the heat to 150°/300°F/Gas 2 and bake for a further hour, or until a skewer inserted into the centre comes out cleanly. Cool in the tin for 10 minutes then turn out to cool on a wire rack.

**Cook's tip:**
Store in an airtight tin for a week to improve the flavour.

# Quick Prep - Slow Cook

As the heading suggests, this chapter is basically about creating meals when you only have a little time available before you need to leave the kitchen. For this you will need either a slow cooker or a good quality casserole pot with a lid. There are some invaluable tips to avoid wasting time: always have your store cupboard well stocked; make sure you have all the vital ingredients defrosted; keep your kitchen uncluttered; use your food processor as it is often quicker than chopping and one we all forget on occasion – preheat your oven! Follow these guidelines and I am sure you will rustle up a great meal, ready to cook in minutes.

# Lamb Hotpot

This must be one of the simplest casserole dishes to put together. You can brown the meat first but I do not find it absolutely necessary.

## Ingredients for 2

250g/9oz lean lamb, cubed
450g/1lb potatoes, sliced
100g/4oz carrots, sliced
100g/4oz parsnips, sliced
150ml/¼pt lamb or beef
  stock
Salt and freshly ground
  black pepper
A little oil for brushing

## Ingredients for 4

500g/1lb 2oz lean lamb,
  cubed
900g/2lb potatoes, sliced
225g/8oz carrots, sliced
225g/8oz parsnips, sliced
300ml/½pt lamb or beef
  stock
Salt and freshly ground
  black pepper
A little oil for brushing

1 Preheat the oven to 180°C/350°F/Gas 4.

2 Layer the meat and vegetables in a deep ovenproof casserole dish, starting and finishing with potato. Lightly season the layers with salt and pepper.

3 Carefully pour the stock over so that it seeps into the layers.

4 Brush the top with a little oil.

5 Bake for 1½–2 hours, until the meat and vegetables are tender.

6 If the top begins to brown too much before the end of the cooking time, cover with foil.

# Pot-roast Chicken

Pot-roasting gives a really succulent roast chicken.

Ingredients for 4-6

1.5kg/3lb free-range chicken
3 tbsp sunflower oil
2 onions, cut into wedges
900g/2lb new potatoes
450ml/¾ pint chicken or vegetable stock
2 tsp cornflour mixed with a little water (optional)
Salt and freshly ground black pepper
Pinch freshly grated nutmeg

1 Preheat the oven to 190°C/375°F/Gas 5. Season the chicken with salt, pepper and a pinch of nutmeg.

2 Heat 2 tbsp of the oil in a large frying pan and brown the chicken on all sides. Transfer to a large ovenproof casserole.

3 Arrange the onions and potatoes around the chicken.

4 Cover and place in the centre of the oven for 1½ hours until the chicken is tender and the juices run clear.

5 Transfer the chicken to a serving plate and keep warm. Remove the vegetables with a draining spoon and keep warm.

6 Spoon any fat from the stock in the pan and thicken with a little cornflour if preferred, or serve as a thin gravy.

7 Serve the chicken with the vegetables and the gravy.

# Creamy Mushroom & Ham Bake

This is an economical family meal. Season lightly with salt as both the ham and cheese contain salt.

## Ingredients for 2

450g/1lb medium floury
  potatoes
75g/3oz button mushrooms,
  sliced
75g/3oz sliced ham, cut
  into strips
1 small onion, thinly sliced
75ml/2½fl oz milk
75g/3oz herb and garlic
  cream cheese
15g/¹/2oz butter
salt and freshly ground
  black pepper

## Ingredients for 4

900g/2lb medium floury
  potatoes
150g/6oz button mushrooms,
  sliced
150g/6oz sliced ham, cut
  into strips
1 large onion, thinly sliced
150ml/5fl oz milk
150g/6oz herb and garlic
  cream cheese
25g/1oz butter
salt and freshly ground
  black pepper

1 Preheat the oven to 180°C/350°F/Gas 4. Grease a shallow ovenproof dish.

2 Parboil the potatoes in boiling water for 5 minutes. Drain and allow to cool slightly. Skin the potatoes and slice thinly. Arrange a layer in the bottom of the dish.

3 Add a layer of mushrooms, ham and onion.

4 Repeat the layers, finishing with a layer of potato.

Lightly season the layers.

5 Heat the milk and cheese in a small pan, stirring until combined. Pour over the potatoes.

6 Dot the top with butter and bake for about 45 minutes, or until the potatoes are tender and the top is golden.

# Sizzling Sausage Bake

This is such an easy supper dish to rustle up after a busy day. Just throw all the ingredients in a roasting tray and put your feet up.

## Ingredients for 2

450g/1lb small new potatoes, quartered
1 clove garlic, crushed
1 tbsp sunflower oil
Sea salt
8 pork chipolata sausages
225g/8oz cherry tomatoes
1 tbsp green pesto

## Ingredients for 4

900g/2lb small new potatoes, quartered
2 cloves garlic, crushed
2 tbsp sunflower oil
Sea salt
16 pork chipolata sausages
450g/1lb cherry tomatoes
2 tbsp green pesto

1 Preheat the oven to 200°C/400°F/Gas 6. Put the potatoes in a large roasting tray with the garlic and oil. Season with sea salt and toss the potato wedges then bake for 10 minutes.

2 Prick the sausages all over with a fork, add to the pan and toss in the oil. Bake for 10 minutes.

3 Add the tomatoes, toss in the pesto and bake for a further 5–10 minutes until the tomatoes and sausages are tender and cooked.

4 Divide between warmed plates and serve with green beans.

# Potato & Chicken Goulash

I love making meals in one pot; it saves on the washing up.

| Ingredients for 2 | Ingredients for 4 |
|---|---|
| 2 tbsp sunflower oil | 3 tbsp sunflower oil |
| 2 chicken portions | 4 chicken portions |
| 1 small onion, peeled and cut into wedges | 1 large onion, peeled and cut into wedges |
| 1 clove garlic, chopped | 2 cloves garlic, chopped |
| 450g/1lb baby new potatoes, halved if large | 900g/2lb baby new potatoes, halved if large |
| 1 tbsp plain flour | 2 tbsp plain flour |
| 2 tsp paprika | 1 tbsp paprika |
| 150ml/¼pt chicken stock | 300ml/½pt chicken stock |
| 2 tsp tomato purée | 1 tbsp tomato purée |
| ½ tsp dried mixed herbs | 1 tsp dried mixed herbs |
| Salt and freshly ground black pepper | Salt and freshly ground black pepper |
| Crème fraîche to serve | Crème fraîche to serve |

1 Heat the oil in a large pan and fry the chicken quickly until browned on all sides. Remove from the pan.

2 Reduce the heat and stir in the onion, cook gently for 3–4 minutes until softened.

3 Add the garlic and potatoes to the pan.

4 Sprinkle with flour and paprika and cook, stirring, for 1 minute.

5 Stir in the stock, tomato purée and herbs. Season with salt and pepper.

6 Return the chicken to the pan. Cover and cook gently for 25–30 minutes until the potatoes are tender and the chicken is done.

7 Serve with a little crème fraîche spooned on top.

# Red-cabbage & Chickpea Bake

This dish tastes even better if it is made the day before it is due to be eaten. Simply prepare it to the end of step 4, let it cool and then chill it in the fridge until you are ready to resume cooking. The next day, start by heating it until it is bubbling hot, then continue with the recipe.

ingredients for 2-3

½ medium-sized red cabbage
25g/1oz butter
½ tbsp olive oil
100g/4oz baby onions,peeled
1 clove garlic, peeled and
    crushed
125g/4½ oz cooking apples,
    peeled and sliced
150ml/¼ pt red wine
50ml/3½ tbsp red wine vinegar
1 heaped tbsp soft,
    dark-brown sugar
1 tsp dried thyme
4 thick slices French bread
1 x 200g/7oz can chickpeas,
    rinsed and drained
Salt and freshly ground
    black pepper

ingredients for 4-6

1 medium-sized red cabbage
50g/2oz butter
1 tbsp olive oil
200g/7oz baby onions, peeled
2 cloves garlic, peeled and
    crushed
250g/9oz cooking apples,
    peeled and sliced
300ml/ /2pt red wine
100ml/3½ fl oz red wine
vinegar
2 heaped tbsp soft,
    dark-brown sugar
2 tsp dried thyme
8 thick slices French bread
1 x 400g/14oz can chickpeas,
    rinsed and drained
Salt and freshly ground
    black pepper

1 Remove any tough outer leaves from the cabbage and discard. Using a large sharp knife cut the cabbage in half from top to bottom. Remove the tough core and discard. Finely shred and set to one side.

2 Preheat the oven to 170°C/325°F/Gas 3. Heat half the butter and all the oil in a large ovenproof casserole. Add the baby onions and cook over a moderate heat until they start to brown.

3 Stir in half the garlic and the apple and cook for 1–2 minutes. Add the shredded cabbage and cook, stirring until well mixed.

4 Pour over the wine and vinegar. Sprinkle with the sugar and herbs and stir well to mix. Cover with a well-fitting lid and place in the oven for 1 hour.

5 Mix the remaining butter with the garlic and spread over the bread slices.

6 Remove the casserole from the oven and stir through the chick peas and season to taste. Top with the buttered bread and return to the oven uncovered for 15 minutes. Serve.

# Meadow Pie

There was much debate in my house about what this dish should be called, as it is loosely based on shepherd's pie, but obviously without the meat. After a lot of discussion, and even more eating, we finally came up with meadow pie.

## ingredients for 2-4

300g/10½ oz potatoes, peeled and cut into chunks
45ml/3 tbsp milk
15g/½ oz butter
1 tbsp wholegrain mustard
Salt and freshly ground black pepper
1 tbsp oil
1 small onion, peeled and chopped
100g/4oz carrots, peeled and diced
1 large stick celery, washed and chopped
100g/4oz whole green lentils, washed and drained
1 x 200g/7oz can chopped tomatoes
1 tsp yeast extract
75ml/5 tbsp vegetable stock
1 tsp dried thyme

## ingredients for 4-8

600g/1lb 5oz potatoes, peeled and cut into chunks
100ml/3½ fl oz milk
25g/1oz butter
2 tbsp wholegrain mustard
Salt and freshly ground black pepper
2 tbsp oil
1 onion, peeled and chopped
225g/8oz carrots, peeled and diced
3 sticks celery, washed and chopped
225g/8oz whole green lentils, washed and drained
1 x 400g/14oz can chopped tomatoes
2 tsp yeast extract
150ml/¼ pt vegetable stock
1 tsp dried thyme

1 Cook the potatoes in a large pan of boiling water for 12–15 minutes or until tender. Drain thoroughly and mash with the milk, butter and mustard. Season to taste. Set to one side until ready to use.

2 Preheat the oven to 190°C/ 375°F/Gas 5. Heat the oil in a large frying pan and cook the onion until golden. Add the carrots and celery and continue to cook, stirring from time to time, for 5 minutes.

3 Add the lentils, tomatoes, yeast extract and vegetable stock, stirring well to mix. Bring gently to the boil. Sprinkle over the thyme and continue to cook at a gentle simmer for 10 minutes. Check the lentils to make sure they are tender. If they are still not tender cook them for a little longer, adding a little water if the mixture is looking too dry. Remove from the heat and season to taste.

4 Spoon the mixture into a large ovenproof dish. Spoon over the mashed potatoes, roughing up the surface with a fork. Bake in the preheated oven for 25 minutes until the top is golden in places and it is piping hot. Serve.

# Mincemeat Cake

Make this cake with ingredients from the store cupboard. It is a great last-minute cake for celebrations, such as anniversaries or Christmas, and keeps well for 2 weeks.

## Ingredients for 12

100g/4oz butter
100g/4oz soft dark
    muscovado sugar
3 eggs, beaten
225g/8oz self-raising flour
1 tsp mixed spice
400g/14oz jar of fruit
    mincemeat
75g/3oz glacé cherries
75g/3oz no-soak prunes,
    chopped
50g/2oz walnut pieces,
    chopped
50g/2oz plain chocolate,
    grated

## Topping

25g/1oz sieved apricot jam
100g/4oz glacé fruits such
as ginger, pineapple,
apricots, cherries

1 Preheat the oven to 160°C/325°F/Gas 3. Grease and double line the base and sides of a 20cm/8in round, deep cake tin with non-stick paper.

2 Beat the butter and sugar together until light and fluffy, then add the egg a little at a time, using a little flour with each addition.

3 Sift the remaining flour and spice into the bowl, then fold in with all the remaining ingredients. Spoon into the tin, make a slight hollow in the centre, then spread the sides level.

4 Bake in the centre of the oven for 1 hour 45 minutes to 2 hours. Test with a skewer – if it comes out cleanly, the cake is done. Cool the cake in the tin.

5 For the topping, brush the cake top with apricot glaze, place the glacé fruits on top in an attractive pattern, and brush again with glaze.

# Strawberries with Mascarpone

This dessert makes the most of luscious summer fruits. To make life simple, you can marinade the strawberries ahead of time.

## Ingredients for 2

225g/8oz fresh, ripe
   strawberries
2 tbsp amaretto or peach
   liqueur
2 tbsp caster sugar
½ the white of 1 large egg
50g/2oz mascarpone cheese
Cocoa powder

## Ingredients for 4

450g/1lb fresh, ripe
   strawberries
4 tbsp amaretto or peach
   liqueur
4 tbsp caster sugar
The white of 1 large egg
100g/4oz mascarpone
   cheese
Cocoa powder

1 Remove the hulls from the strawberries and toss in the liqueur with half the sugar. Chill for 10 minutes.

2 Whisk the egg white to soft peaks, add the remaining sugar and whisk again to form floppy peaks.

3 Fold a spoonful of the egg white into the cheese to slacken it, then fold in the remaining egg white gently.

4 Divide the strawberries and their juices between glass serving dishes. Top each with the mascarpone cream and sprinkle with cocoa powder.

# Chocolate Bread & Butter Puddings

The puffy croissant layers, packed with sticks of chocolate make lovely little hot puddings.

## Ingredients for 2

- 15g/½ oz butter
- 2 chocolate croissants or pains au chocolat
- 1 egg
- 5 tbsp milk
- 6 tbsp single cream
- ½ tsp vanilla extract
- 25g/1oz caster sugar
- 4 tsp demerara sugar

## Ingredients for 4

- 25g/1oz butter
- 4 chocolate croissants or pains au chocolat
- 2 eggs
- 125ml/4fl oz milk
- 150ml/5fl oz single cream
- 1 tsp vanilla extract
- 50g/2oz caster sugar
- 8 tsp demerara sugar

1 Preheat the oven to 190°C/375°F/Gas 5. Thickly butter 2 (4) 600ml/1pt ovenproof dishes and place them in a small roasting tin.

2 Cut the chocolate croissants into 2 cm/¾in thick slices and arrange, overlapping, in the dishes. Beat the eggs then whisk together with the milk, cream, essence and caster sugar.

3 Pour the custard over the slices, then sprinkle the top of each with 2 tsp of demerara sugar.

4 Pour boiling water into the tin to come halfway up the sides of the dishes. Bake for 20 minutes until golden brown and firm.

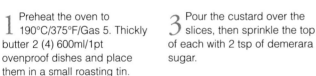

# Feeling Thrifty

Whatever reason you have for trying to budget, and whether it's just for one meal or more long-term, there are plenty of ways to make changes that can give immediate results. Nowadays farmers markets are well established and you can usually buy almost everything you need for weekly household cooking. They can be much more enjoyable – and cheaper – than supermarkets, especially for vegetables. Meat can take up a large proportion of a weekly budget, so try limiting it to two or three times per week – it's surprisingly easy to take inspiration from other key ingredients.

# Savoury Potato Scones with Cheese & Chives

Serve these yummy savoury scones as part of a packed lunch or with a meal, in place of bread.

## Ingredients for 2

25g/1oz butter
75g/3oz self-raising flour
50g/2oz Cheshire cheese,
    grated
1 tbsp snipped fresh chives
100g/4oz cold mashed potato
1 to 2 tbsp milk, plus extra
    for brushing

## Ingredients for 4

50g/2oz butter
175g/6oz self-raising flour
100g/4 oz Cheshire cheese,
    grated
2 tbsp snipped fresh chives
225g/8oz cold mashed potato
2 to 3 tbsp milk plus extra for
brushing

1 Preheat oven to 200°C/400°F/Gas 6.

2 Rub the butter into the flour, until the mixture resembles fine breadcrumbs.

3 Stir in most of the cheese and chives. Add the mashed potato and mix well. Add enough milk to bring the mixture together to form a soft dough.

4 Roll out the dough to about 2cm/³/₄in thick and cut out 7.5cm/3in scones using a round cookie cutter. Place on a lightly greased baking sheet.

5 Brush the tops with a little extra milk and sprinkle the remaining cheese on top. Bake for 20 minutes or until risen and golden. Serve warm.

# Oven-baked Tuna Risotto

Put all the ingredients into one pot and pop it into the oven – it couldn't be easier

## Ingredients for 2

1 tbsp olive oil
1 small onion, finely
    chopped
100g/4oz risotto rice
175ml/6fl oz vegetable stock
200g/7oz canned chopped
    tomatoes
185g/6½ oz can tuna in oil,
    drained
2 courgettes, coarsely grated
Salt
Black pepper, freshly ground
½ tsp dried oregano
25g/1oz Parmesan cheese,
    shaved into curls
1 tbsp fresh flat-leaf parsley,
    chopped

## Ingredients for 4

2 tbsp olive oil
1 large onion, finely chopped
200g/7oz risotto rice
375ml/12fl oz vegetable
    stock
400g/14oz can chopped
    tomatoes
2 x 185g/6½ oz cans tuna in
    oil, drained
4 courgettes, coarsely grated
Salt
Black pepper, freshly ground
1 tsp dried oregano
50g/2oz Parmesan cheese,
    shaved into curls
2 tbsp fresh flat-leaf parsley,
    chopped

1 Preheat the oven to 200°C/400°F/Gas 6. Heat the olive oil in a large frying pan, add the onion and cook until soft.

2 Add the rice, stock and tomatoes and bring to a simmer. Stir in the tuna and courgettes and season with salt, freshly ground black pepper and the herbs. Transfer to a heatproof casserole.

3 Place on the lid or cover the pot tightly with a sheet of foil and bake for 25 minutes until the rice is tender.

4 Divide between warmed serving bowls and scatter with curls of Parmesan cheese and fresh parsley.

# Vegetable Potato Pie

A great midweek family meal, this is a very versatile recipe. Use whatever vegetables you have to hand. You can even add cooked vegetables left over from another meal. If you like, you can add some chunks of fish to the sauce as well.

## Ingredients for 2

1 carrot, thickly sliced
75g/3oz swede or pumpkin,
    cut into chunks
75g/3oz cauliflower florets
75g/3oz broccoli florets
25g/1oz frozen peas
25g/1oz frozen sweetcorn
    niblets
15g/½ oz butter
15g/½ oz flour
225ml/8fl oz milk
1 tsp Dijon mustard
350g/12oz floury potatoes,
    peeled
75g/3oz red Leicester
    cheese, grated
Salt and freshly ground
    black pepper

## Ingredients for 4

2 carrots, thickly sliced
175g/6oz swede or pumpkin,
    cut into chunks
175g/6oz cauliflower florets
175g/6oz broccoli florets
50g/2oz frozen peas
50g/2oz frozen sweetcorn
    niblets
25g/1oz butter
25g/1oz flour
450ml/¾ pt milk
1 tbsp Dijon mustard
700g/1½ lb floury potatoes,
    peeled
175g/6oz red Leicester
    cheese, grated
Salt and freshly ground
    black pepper

1 Preheat the oven to 190°C/375°F/Gas 5. Bring a pan of water to the boil and add the carrots and swede. Return to the boil and cook for 3 minutes.

2 Add the cauliflower and broccoli and cook for a further 3–5 minutes until the vegetables are just tender.

3 Add the peas and sweetcorn and remove from the heat. Drain and tip into a shallow ovenproof dish.

4 Melt the butter in a small saucepan and stir in the flour. Cook for 1 minute.

5 Remove from the heat and gradually beat in the milk. Return to the heat and cook, stirring constantly, until the sauce thickens slightly. Stir in the mustard and season with salt and pepper.

6 Pour the sauce over the vegetables and level the top.

7 Parboil the potatoes for 5 minutes. Drain and allow to cool slightly.

8 Grate the potatoes and toss with the cheese. Pile on top of the vegetables and bake for 45 minutes until the top is crisp and golden.

# Mushroom & Ale Pie

I first tasted this pie in a traditional English pub. Make sure that you serve it with plenty of bread or potatoes to soak up all of that lovely, rich gravy.

## ingredients for 2

1 onion, peeled
300g/10½ oz mushrooms
15g/½ oz butter
½ tbsp oil
1 small clove garlic, peeled and crushed
½ stick celery, sliced
2 tbsp plain flour
150ml/¼pt brown ale
1 tsp Dijon mustard
1 tbsp fresh parsley, chopped
Salt and freshly ground black pepper
250g/9oz puff pastry
1 beaten egg, small

## ingredients for 4

2 onions, peeled
600g/1lb 2oz mushrooms
25g/1oz butter
1 tbsp oil
1 clove garlic, peeled and crushed
1 stick celery, sliced
4 tbsp plain flour
300ml/½ pt brown ale
2 tsp Dijon mustard
2 tbsp fresh parsley, chopped
Salt and freshly ground black pepper
500g/1lb 2oz puff pastry
1 beaten egg

1 Using a sharp knife slice the onions into thin wedges. Thickly slice the mushrooms. If some are small leave them whole.

2 Heat oil and butter in a large pan and cook the onions and garlic over a moderate heat until they soften. Add the celery and cook for a further 2–3 minutes.

3 Add the mushrooms and stir well to coat in the onion and celery mixture. Cover and cook over a gentle heat, stirring from time to time until the mushrooms change colour and soften (about 10 minutes).

4 Sprinkle over the flour and cook, stirring, for 1 minute, until all the flour is mixed in and any juices that have collected are absorbed.

5 Add a little of the ale and stir well to mix; it will thicken quite quickly at this point. Continue adding the ale a little at a time until it is all incorporated. Simmer gently for 5 minutes. Remove from the heat. Stir in the mustard and parsley and season to taste. Pour into a 600ml/1pt (1.2l/2pt) deep pie dish. If using individual ones, divide the mixture equally between them. Set to one side to cool a little.

6 Preheat the oven to 200°C/400°F/Gas 6. Roll out the pastry on a well-floured surface to approximately 1cm/½in thick. Brush the edges of the pie dish with a little water. Cut thin strips of pastry and press them around the edge of the pie dish. Brush this pastry edge with a little more water. Now take the larger piece of pastry and drape over the pie dish, then cut away the excess. Use the pastry scraps to decorate the top of the pie, if you wish. Brush with beaten egg to glaze. Using a sharp knife cut 2–3, 3cm/2in slashes in the middle of the pastry to allow steam to escape during cooking.

7 Bake in the preheated oven for 25–30 minutes. Serve with crusty bread or potatoes and a vegetable of your choice.

# Pot-Roast Brisket

This recipe is a great meal to make after a trip to the farmers market, for both the meat and vegetables. I like brisket as it is an economical joint for this dish, but if your stall doesn't have brisket, ask the stallholder what other meat they would recommend. It is a good chance to make friends with your supplier. I often make this into two meals, serving the meat hot with the vegetables and gravy on day one, and then cold the following day accompanied by chips and tomatoes, or jacket potatoes and beans.

## Ingredients for 8

1.3kg/3lb rolled brisket
225g/8oz shallots or small onions
700g/1½ lb mixed root vegetables, such as carrots, parsnips,
    swede and turnips
25g/1oz beef dripping or 2 tbsp sunflower oil
300ml/½ pint beef stock
Few sprigs fresh thyme
2 bay leaves
175g/6oz button mushrooms (optional)
Salt and freshly ground black pepper

1 Preheat the oven to 170°C/325°F/Gas 3. Season the brisket. If using onions, cut into quarters. Peel and cut the root vegetables into large chunks.

2 Heat the dripping or oil in a large flameproof casserole and brown the meat on all sides. You may find it easier to brown the meat in a frying pan and transfer it to a casserole dish.

3 Add the root vegetables, stock, thyme and bay leaf. Cover and cook for 2 hours.

4 Add the mushrooms (if using) and return to the oven for another 30 minutes.

5 Slice the meat and surround with vegetables. Spoon gravy over, or serve separately.

# Chick-peas & Potatoes

This curry is a perfect, quick midweek meal to serve with rice or bread.

## ingredients for 2

1 tbsp oil
1 medium onion, peeled and
    chopped
½ tsp fennel
½ tsp whole coriander
1 tsp whole cumin
¼ tsp turmeric
2 cloves garlic
½ green chilli
2.5cm/1in fresh ginger,
peeled and finely grated
400g/14oz can chick peas
225g/8oz waxy potatoes,
    cooked, cooled and diced
1 tbsp lemon juice
200g/7oz can tomatoes,
    chopped
Salt and freshly ground
    black pepper
Cayenne pepper and yoghurt
    to serve

## ingredients for 4

2 tbsp oil
1 large onion, peeled and
    chopped
1 tsp fennel
1 tsp whole coriander
2 tsp whole cumin
½ tsp turmeric
4 cloves garlic
1 green chilli
5cm/2in fresh ginger, peeled
    and finely grated
2 x 400g/14oz can chick peas
450g/1lb waxy potatoes,
    cooked, cooled and diced
2 tbsp lemon juice
400g/14oz can chopped
    tomatoes
Salt and freshly ground
    black pepper
Cayenne pepper and yoghurt
    to serve

1 Heat the oil in a large frying
pan and cook the onion
until it becomes transparent.
Dry roast the whole spices in a
small frying pan for 2–3
minutes or until they smell
toasted and fragrant, remove
from the heat and grind.

2 Add all the spices to the
onions along with the
garlic, chilli and ginger and
cook, stirring for 2 minutes.

3 Stir in the chick-peas and
potatoes and mix well to
coat them with the spiced
onion mixture. Cook for 3–4
minutes.

4 Pour over the tomatoes,
bring to a gentle simmer
and cook covered for 10
minutes. Add the lemon juice
and season according to taste.
Serve with a little plain yoghurt
and a small pinch of cayenne
pepper if desired.

# Sausage, Tomato & Pasta Supper

Use good-quality sausages for best results in this great supper dish. Serve topped with a poached egg if desired.

| Ingredients for 2 | Ingredients for 4 |
|---|---|
| 225g/8oz good-quality sausages | 450g/1lb good-quality sausages |
| 100g/4oz cherry tomatoes, halved | 225g/8oz cherry tomatoes, halved |
| 1–2 tbsp olive oil | 3 tbsp olive oil |
| $1/4$ tsp dried sage | $1/2$ tsp dried sage |
| 200g/7oz pasta | 400g/14oz pasta |
| 2 eggs (optional) | 4 eggs (optional) |
| 75g/3oz Cheddar cheese, grated | 175g/6oz Cheddar cheese, grated |
| Salt and freshly ground black pepper | Salt and freshly ground black pepper |

1 Preheat the oven to 190°C/375°F/Gas mark 5. Place the sausages on a baking sheet and bake in the oven for 15 minutes.

2 Cut the cherry tomatoes in half and place around the sausages. Sprinkle with sage and drizzle with a little of the olive oil. Season with salt and pepper. Return to the oven for 15 minutes or until the sausages are cooked through.

3 Meanwhile, cook the pasta in plenty of lightly salted boiling water for 10 minutes, or as directed on the packet.

4 Poach the eggs (if using) in lightly simmering water for about 4 minutes until just set.

5 When the sausages are cooked, toss the tomatoes into a bowl. Thickly slice the sausages, and add to the tomatoes with the remaining oil.

6 Add the pasta and toss to combine. Serve topped with the poached egg and grated cheese.

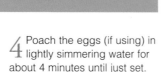

# Coriander & Lentil Soup

Lentils are not only cheap but also full of fibre and protein.

## Ingredients for 2

½ tbsp sunflower oil
1 onion, peeled and finely
    chopped
1 small clove garlic, peeled
    and crushed
1.25cm-/½ in-piece fresh root
    ginger, peeled and finely
    grated
75g/3oz red lentils, washed
600ml/1pt vegetable stock
3 tbsp fresh coriander,
chopped
Salt and freshly ground
    black pepper

## Ingredients for 4

1 tbsp sunflower oil
1 large onion, peeled and
    finely chopped
1 clove garlic, peeled and
    crushed
2.5cm-/1in-piece fresh root
    ginger, peeled and finely
    grated
175g/6oz red lentils, washed
    and drained
1.2l/2pt vegetable stock
6 tbsp fresh coriander,
chopped
Salt and freshly ground
    black pepper

1 Heat the oil in a large saucepan over a moderate heat and cook the onion and garlic until softened. Add the ginger and cook for 1–2 minutes stirring.

2 Stir in the washed and drained lentils mixing well to coat in the onion and oil mixture.

3 Pour over the vegetable stock and bring to the boil. Reduce the heat to a gentle simmer and cook for 30 minutes stirring from time to time.

4 Remove from the heat and stir through the chopped coriander. Season to taste. If you prefer a smoother soup you can blend it in a food processor or blender at this point. Serve with chunks of bread.

# Swiss Roll

A Swiss roll is such a handy cake – make it from store cupboard ingredients in a morning ready for afternoon visitors. It contains no fat at all, so you can go mad and serve it with lashings of clotted cream and strawberries.

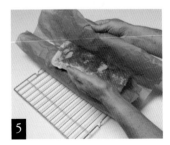

**Ingredients for 18:**

3 large eggs
100g/4oz caster sugar
100g/4oz plain flour
6 tbsp seedless raspberry jam, warmed
Icing sugar to dredge

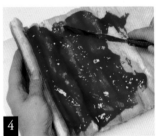

1 Preheat the oven to 200°C/400°F/Gas 6. Grease and line a 33x23cm/13x9in Swiss roll tin with a sheet of non-stick baking paper, 5cm/2in larger than the tin. Snip the corners to fit.

2 Place the eggs and caster sugar in a heatproof bowl and set over a pan of hot water. Whisk with an electric mixer until very thick and pale. The mixer should leave a trail when the beaters are lifted away. Remove from the pan and whisk until cold and thick.

3 Sift half the flour into the mixture and fold in carefully. Sift in the remaining flour and fold in with 1 tbsp of warm water. Spread into the tin and smooth level into all the corners. Bake for 10 minutes, or until golden and firm to the touch.

4 While the sponge is baking, spread a dampened tea towel on a flat surface, lay a large sheet of non-stick paper on top of this and sprinkle with caster sugar. Turn the cooked sponge out on to the sugared paper and trim away the crusty edges. Spread with the warmed jam.

5 Roll up the sponge, using the paper as a guide. Leave the cake to cool wrapped up in the paper to prevent it from unrolling. To serve, remove the paper and dust with icing sugar.

# BLB cupcakes

In our family, these are known as 'boring little buns'. Why, I have no idea, as they are totally delicious when still warm from the oven with a hot cup of coffee – ideal for an easy, coffee-break snack.

## Ingredients for 12 cakes

100g/4oz butter
100g/4oz caster sugar
2 eggs, beaten
100g/4oz self-raising flour
Makes 11 cupcakes (approx)

1 Preheat the oven to 200°C/400°F/Gas 6, then line a 12-hole bun tin with paper cases.

2 Cream the butter and the sugar until pale and fluffy. Add the eggs a little at a time, beating well after each addition. Using a metal spoon, fold in the flour. If the mixture is too dry, add a little milk to make it a soft, dropping consistency. Alternatively, put all of the ingredients (apart from the milk) into a food processor, whiz until smooth, and then add the milk.

3 Spoon the mixture into the paper cases and bake for 15–20 minutes, or until risen and firm on the top. Transfer to a wire rack to cool.

# Healthy Eating

Healthy eating should never be dull – quite the opposite in fact. These inspiring farmhouse-style recipes still deliver on flavour but have all the ingredients to energise without excessive fat or sugar. The contents of this chapter have ideas for juicing, healthy comfort food and nourishing snacks, which shows you can obtain a happy medium without sacrificing anything in the way of taste.

# Chicken Spiced Rice

This is just as tasty hot or cold. Handy to pack in lunch boxes

## Ingredients for 2

125g/5oz basmati rice
2 tsp sunflower oil
1 small onion, peeled and
    sliced into thin wedges
1 clove garlic, peeled and
    finely chopped
½-1 fresh red chilli
    according to taste
1cm/½ in ginger, peeled and
    finely grated
125g/4½ oz carrots, peeled
    and coarsely grated
½ yellow pepper, deseeded
    thinly sliced
1 medium courgette, trimmed
    and sliced into thin batons
½ tbsp paprika
1 large chicken breast,
cooked and shredded
1½ tbsp tomato ketchup
½ tbsp dark soy sauce
Fresh coriander to garnish
Freshly ground black pepper
    to taste

## Ingredients for 4

250g/9oz basmati rice
4 tsp sunflower oil
1 onion, peeled and sliced
    into thin wedges
2 cloves garlic, peeled and
    finely chopped
1-2 fresh red chillies
    according to taste
2.5cm/1in ginger, peeled and
    finely grated
250g/9oz carrots, peeled and
    coarsely grated
1 yellow pepper, deseeded
    and thinly sliced
1 large courgette, trimmed
    and sliced into thin batons
1 tbsp paprika
2 large chicken breasts,
    cooked and shredded
3 tbsp tomato ketchup
1 tbsp dark soy sauce
Fresh coriander to garnish
Freshly ground black pepper
    to taste

1 Rinse the rice under cold running water and drain thoroughly. Now place the rice in a saucepan with 300ml/½pt (600ml/1pt) water and bring to the boil. Reduce the heat to a gentle simmer and cover with a well-fitting lid. Cook for 8–10 minutes or until all the liquid has been absorbed. Fork through to separate the rice and set to one side while you prepare the rest of the dish.

2 Heat the oil in a wok or large frying pan and cook the onion until it softens. Add the garlic, chilli and ginger and continue to cook, stirring, for 2–3 minutes.

1

**3** Stir in the carrots, pepper and courgette. Stir-fry for 3–4 minutes. Sprinkle over the paprika and cook for 1 minute. Add the cooked rice and mix thoroughly. Stir in the shredded chicken.

**4** Mix the tomato ketchup and soy sauce with 1 (2) tbsp water and pour over the rice mixture, stirring as you do so. Continue to cook, stirring, for 5 minutes until the mixture is piping hot. Season to taste and serve garnished with coriander.

# Potato Moussaka

Moussaka is a classic Greek dish, which is usually made with layers of aubergine. Here, it has been adapted to use potatoes, which absorb less oil, making it a lower fat alternative to the traditional version.

### Ingredients for 2

300g/10½ oz potatoes,
    peeled and thinly sliced
2 tsp olive oil
1 small onion, finely chopped
1 clove garlic, chopped
250g/9oz lean minced beef
1 heaped tbsp tomato purée
2 tbsp red wine or water
25g/1oz butter
25g/1oz plain flour
300ml/½ pt milk
1 egg
75g/3oz Cheddar cheese,
    grated
Salt and ground pepper

### Ingredients for 4

500g/1lb 2oz potatoes,
    peeled and thinly sliced
1 tbsp olive oil
1 onion, finely chopped
2 cloves garlic, chopped
500g/1lb 2oz lean
    minced beef
3 tbsp tomato purée
4 tbsp red wine or water
50g/2oz butter
50g/2oz plain flour
600ml/1pt milk
2 eggs
75g/3oz Cheddar cheese,
    grated
Salt and ground pepper

1 Preheat the oven to 190°C/375°F/Gas 5. Lightly grease a baking dish.

2 Blanch the potatoes in boiling water for 3 minutes. Drain.

3 Heat the oil in a frying pan and fry the onion and garlic until soft. Add the mince and cook until browned, breaking it up as it cooks.

4 Stir in the tomato purée and red wine or water. Season with salt and pepper. Remove from the heat and set aside.

5 Melt the butter in a saucepan, stir in the flour, cook for 30 seconds and remove from the heat.

6 Gradually stir in the milk and return to the heat. Cook, stirring constantly, until the sauce thickens. Season well.

7 Lightly beat the eggs to break up. Beat them into the white sauce.

8 Layer potato and meat mixture alternately in the dish, finishing with a layer of potato.

9 Pour sauce over the top and sprinkle with grated cheese. Bake in the centre of the oven for 45 minutes.

# Warm Tuna & Roasted Pepper Salad

Fresh tuna is rich in omega-3 fatty acids, which have numerous health benefits.

## Ingredients for 2

- 1½ mixed sweet peppers
- 1 tbsp olive oil
- 300g/10½oz new potatoes
- 1 tsp red wine vinegar
- 1 tsp wholegrain mustard
- 2 x 150g/5oz tuna steaks

## Ingredients for 4

- 3 mixed sweet peppers
- 2 tbsp olive oil
- 600g/1lb 5oz new potatoes
- 2 tsp red wine vinegar
- 2 tsp wholegrain mustard
- 4 x 150g/5oz tuna steaks

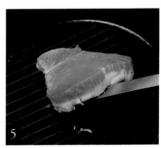

1 Preheat the oven to 200°C/400°F/Gas 6. Halve the peppers, deseed and cut into slices. Place the sliced peppers in a mixing bowl, drizzle over a third of the olive oil and toss well to coat.

2 Spread the peppers in a single layer over a large baking tray and cook in the preheated oven for 25 minutes, turning them once halfway through.

3 Bring a large pan of water to the boil and cook the new potatoes for approximately 10 minutes until they are tender. Drain and set aside.

4 Whisk the remaining oil with the vinegar in a small mixing bowl. Add the mustard and whisk again.

5 Preheat a griddle pan over a moderately high heat and cook the tuna steaks for about 4–5 minutes each side, until piping hot. Remove from the heat.

6 To serve, mix the roasted pepper strips with the new potatoes and drizzle over the mustard dressing. Roughly flake the tuna and add to the potatoes and peppers. Toss lightly to mix and divide between the serving plates while still warm.

# Creamy Tomato & Thyme Shells

Ricotta is a relatively low-fat cheese and is a good source of calcium and protein.

## Ingredients for 2

2 tsp olive oil
1 small onion, peeled and
  finely chopped
2 cloves garlic, peeled and
  finely chopped
1 x 400g/14oz can tomatoes,
  chopped
Sprig of fresh thyme, plus
  a few leaves for garnish
200g/7oz pasta shells
100g/4oz ricotta
Black pepper

## Ingredients for 4

4 tsp olive oil
1 large onion, peeled and
  finely chopped
4 cloves garlic, peeled and
  finely chopped
2 x 400g/14oz cans tomatoes,
  chopped
Large sprig of fresh thyme,
  plus a few leaves for
  garnish
400g/14oz pasta shells
200g/7oz ricotta
Black pepper

1 Heat the oil in a frying pan over a moderate heat and cook the onion until soft. Add the garlic and cook for 2 minutes, stirring. Pour in the tomatoes and bring gently to the boil.

2 Add the thyme and reduce the heat to a gentle simmer. Cook for about 15 minutes until the mixture thickens.

3 Bring a large pan of water to the boil and cook the pasta according to the packet instructions. Drain.

4 Add the ricotta to the thickened tomato and cook for a further 5 minutes. Divide the pasta between the serving plates and spoon over the sauce. Season with black pepper and garnish with fresh thyme leaves. Serve.

# Frittata

This thick omelette is packed with potatoes, beans and peppers. It can be served either on its own or with a light salad.

## Ingredients for 2-3

175g/ 6oz new potatoes
50g/2oz green beans, trimmed and cut into 5cm/2in lengths
1 tbsp olive oil
1 red onion, peeled and finely chopped
1/2 red pepper, chopped
1/2 orange pepper, chopped
1 clove garlic, peeled and crushed
75g/3oz courgettes, chopped
3 eggs
Salt and freshly ground black pepper
50g/2oz pitted black olives
40g/1½oz Parmesan cheese, finely grated

## Ingredients for 4-6

350g/12oz new potatoes
100g/4oz green beans, trimmed and cut into 5cm/2in lengths
2 tbsp olive oil
1 large red onion, peeled and finely chopped
1 red pepper, chopped
1 orange pepper, chopped
2 cloves garlic, peeled and crushed
175g/6oz courgettes, chopped
6 eggs
Salt and freshly ground black pepper
100g/4oz pitted black olives
75g/3oz Parmesan cheese, finely grated

1 Scrub the potatoes and cut into bite-size chunks if large. Bring a large pan of water to the boil and add the potatoes. Cook for about 10 minutes or until just tender. Add the beans and cook for a further 2 minutes, drain and set to one side.

2 Meanwhile heat the oil in a large frying pan and cook the onions until golden in places. Add the peppers and cook for 5 minutes, stirring from time to time. Add the drained potatoes and the garlic. Continue to cook, stirring from time to time, until the peppers are softened and the potatoes are starting to get golden in places.

3 Add the courgettes and beans and stir-fry for 3–4 minutes or until the courgettes are tender. Beat the eggs together and season with salt and pepper.

4 Pour the eggs over the vegetables, tilting the pan to spread them evenly through the vegetables. Sprinkle the olives over the top.

5 Preheat the grill to moderate. Cook gently on the stove top for approximately 5 minutes or until set. Sprinkle with the Parmesan cheese and place under the preheated grill for 3–4 minutes. Serve cut in wedges on its own, or with a light salad.

# Bean Burgers

There are many recipes for bean burgers, but here is the one that I like to cook. If you prefer to use only one variety of beans, then do so. Serve the bean burgers with a light salad or even sandwiched in a bun with chips.

## Ingredients for 2

½ tbsp oil
½ small onion, peeled and
    finely chopped
1 small clove garlic, peeled
    and crushed
½ tsp chilli powder
½ tsp ground cumin
1 x 200g/7oz can red kidney
    beans
1 x 200g/7oz can cannellini
    beans
½ tbsp tomato purée
2 tbsp plain flour
25g/1oz fresh brown
    breadcrumbs
Salt and freshly ground
    black pepper
1 egg, beaten
Dried breadcrumbs for
    coating
Oil for frying

## Ingredients for 4

1 tbsp oil
1 small onion, peeled and
    finely chopped
1 clove garlic, peeled and
    crushed
1 tsp chilli powder
1 tsp ground cumin
1 x 400g/14oz can red kidney
    beans
1 x 400g/14oz can cannellini
    beans
1 tbsp tomato purée
4 tbsp plain flour
50g/2oz fresh brown
    breadcrumbs
Salt and freshly ground
    black pepper to taste
2 eggs, beaten
Dried breadcrumbs for
    coating
Oil for frying

1 Heat the oil in a small frying pan and cook the onions and garlic over a moderate heat until they become softened. Add the chilli powder and cumin and cook for a further minute, stirring.

2 Drain the beans and rinse well under cold running water. Leave to stand and drain for 5 minutes. Remove ¾ of the beans and mash well until almost smooth. This can be done quite easily with a potato masher. Using a fork, very roughly break up the remaining beans and then add to the smooth beans.

3 Stir in the tomato purée, and sautéed onion mixture, stirring well to mix. Sprinkle over the flour and breadcrumbs and season lightly with salt and pepper. Stir. Mix in enough beaten egg to make a firm mixture. Using damp hands divide the mixture into 2 (4) and shape into large patties. Chill in the fridge for 30 minutes minimum.

5 Heat about 1cm/½in of oil in a frying pan over a moderately high heat. Once the oil is hot, carefully place the burgers in the oil and cook for 3–4 minutes on each side until golden and crisp. Remove from the pan using a fish slice. Drain on kitchen paper and serve with a light salad.

4 Place the remaining beaten egg in a shallow dish and the breadcrumbs in another. Dip the chilled burgers first in the beaten egg and then in the dried breadcrumbs, turning to coat.

# Highland Fling

It seems amazing that the most jewel-like, luscious raspberries are often the product of the chilly countryside of northern Europe.

| Ingredients for 2 | Ingredients for 4 |
|---|---|
| 250g/9oz rasberries | 500g/1lb rasberries |
| 1 lemon | 2 lemons |
| 100ml/2fl oz sparkling water | 200ml/4fl oz sparkling water |

Reserve two slices of the lemon for decoration and peel the rest. Rinse the raspberries and juice them, followed by the lemon. Mix the juices together in a glass and top up with sparkling water. Garnish with the lemon slices and maybe a few raspberries.

# Spiced Poached Pears

This low-fat pudding is very simple to prepare.

**Ingredients for 2**
½ tbsp granulated sugar
1 star anise
½ anilla pod, split
½ small cinnamon stick
½ orange
1 large ripe pears
Crème fraîche to serve

**Ingredients for 4**
1 tbsp granulated sugar
2 star anise
1 vanilla pod, split
1 small cinnamon stick
1 orange
2 large ripe pears
Crème fraîche to serve

1 Place the sugar in large saucepan with 150ml/¼pt (300ml/½pt) cold water. Add the star anise, vanilla pod and cinnamon stick.

2 Zest the orange using a zester. Alternatively, using a sharp knife, cut thin strips from the orange skin, ensuring you do not get any of the white pith. Add the zest to the pan, along with the juice from the orange.

3 Bring gently to the boil, stirring from time to ensure that the sugar is fully dissolved. Peel, halve and core the pears. Add to the spiced orange syrup in the pan. Cook, covered, at a gentle simmer for 20 minutes, turning the pears from time to time to ensure they are cooked through.

4 To serve, place a pear half on each plate and keep warm. Bring the cooking liquid back to a rapid boil and cook for 3–4 minutes to reduce by about half. Remove from the heat. Spoon the spiced syrup over the pears, along with a little crème fraîche.

# Granny Smith Sorbet

A delicious tangy dessert, which requires the use of an ice-cream maker.

*Ingredients*
125g/5oz granulated sugar
1 tablespoon liquid glucose
8–10 Granny Smith apples

1 Place the sugar in a large saucepan along with 125ml/4fl oz cold water. Cook over a gentle heat, stirring from time to time, until the sugar has dissolved. Increase the heat until the mixture is boiling. Remove from the heat, stir in the glucose, then leave until completely cool.

2 Wash, quarter and core the apples (do not remove the skins as they give the sorbet its wonderful colour) then juice them. (If you don't have a juicer you can blend them in a food processor or blender, then strain through a fine mesh sieve, pressing down on the pulp to extract as much of the juice as possible.) You need approximately 500ml/1pt of juice. Add the juice to the cooled syrup and stir well to mix. Following the instructions of your ice cream maker use the mixture to make the sorbet.

# Vanilla Rice Pudding

This is delicious hot or at room temperature.

Ingredients for 2

½ vanilla pod
30g/1¼ oz brown rice
25g/1oz pudding rice
300ml/½pt semi-skimmed milk
1 tbsp golden caster sugar
65g/2½ oz French soft prunes, chopped

Ingredients for 4

1 vanilla pod
60g/2½ oz brown rice
50g/2oz pudding rice
600ml/1pt semi-skimmed milk
40g/1½ oz golden caster sugar
125g/4½ oz French soft prunes, chopped

1 Using a sharp knife, split the vanilla pod to reveal the seeds inside. Place the vanilla pod in a large saucepan with a well-fitting lid.

2 Rinse the brown rice thoroughly, then drain and add to the pan along with the pudding rice. Pour over the milk and place over a moderate heat. Bring gently to the boil, reduce the heat to a gentle simmer, cover and

cook, stirring from time to time, for 40–45 minutes until the rice is tender.

3 Remove from the heat and stir in the sugar. Carefully remove the vanilla pod. Gently fold through the chopped prunes and serve hot or at room temperature.

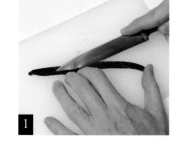

# Exciting Recipes for Children

We all know children love getting messy in the kitchen whilst making tasty food. These are great recipes as they involve lots of hands on preparation and include colourful ingredients that blend magically into delicious smoothies and healthy pizza toppings that can be used to create a smiley face. Whatever keeps your child's attention is important, whether it's planting a few herb seeds and later cooking with them, or crumbling cookie dough (usually on the floor!)

# Sultana Cookies

Succulent sultanas in a crunchy cookie – heaven!

Ingredients for 12 cookies

125g/5oz butter
150g/6oz caster sugar
2 egg yolks
225g/9oz plain flour
Grated rind of one orange
50g/2oz sultanas

1 Preheat the oven to 180°C/350°F/Gas 4. Grease and line two baking sheets with greaseproof paper.

2 To make the biscuits, place the butter and sugar in a bowl and beat together until pale and fluffy. Add the egg yolk, and beat well.

3 Add the flour, sultanas and orange rind and mix well. On a lightly floured surface, knead the mixture lightly and roll out to ½ cm/¼in thickness. Cut into rounds and place on the prepared baking trays.

Bake for 15 minutes until a golden colour.

# Spaghetti & Meatballs

Ideal for a hearty midweek meal, this dish is a firm favourite in my household.

## Ingredients for 2

- 250g/9oz extra lean minced beef
- 15g/½ oz fresh white breadcrumbs
- 1 small shallot, finely chopped
- 1 clove garlic, chopped
- 1 slice pancetta or streaky bacon, chopped
- ½ tsp dried oregano
- 1 tbsp grated Parmesan cheese
- 1 egg yolk
- 1 tbsp olive oil
- 2 tbsp red wine (optional)
- 250g/9oz passata
- 225g/8oz spaghetti
- Salt and freshly ground black pepper
- Grated fresh Parmesan cheese, to serve

## Ingredients for 4

- 500g/1lb 2oz extra lean minced beef
- 25g/1oz fresh white breadcrumbs
- 1 shallot, finely chopped
- 2 cloves garlic, chopped
- 2 slices pancetta or streaky bacon, chopped
- 1 tsp dried oregano
- 2 tbsp grated Parmesan cheese
- 2 egg yolks
- 2 tbsp olive oil
- 4 tbsp red wine (optional)
- 500g/1lb 2oz passata
- 450g/1lb spaghetti
- Salt and freshly ground black pepper
- Grated fresh Parmesan cheese, to serve

1 Mix the beef, crumbs, shallot, garlic, pancetta, oregano, cheese and egg yolk together and seasoning until well blended.

2 Form into about 18–20 small balls. Heat the oil in a large frying pan and fry the balls until browned on all sides.

3 Add the red wine if using, then stir in the passata.

Bring to the boil and simmer, covered, for 20 minutes.

4 Cook the spaghetti in plenty of lightly salted boiling water for 10 minutes, or as directed on the packet.

5 Drain the pasta and divide between serving plates. Spoon the meatballs and sauce on top and serve with a sprinkling of Parmesan cheese.

# Chicken Nuggets with Tomato Sauce

A perennial children's favourite, these nuggets are are much healthier – and tastier – option than those bought in the shops.

## Ingredients for 2

225g/8oz ripe tomatoes
½ small onion
Small clove garlic
½ tsp tomato purée
½ tsp basil (fresh or dried)
1 tsp olive oil
Salt and pepper
2½ tbsp dairy-free margarine
1½ tsp Worcestershire sauce
450g/1lb chicken breast
100g/4oz plain crisps

## Ingredients for 4

450g/1lb ripe tomatoes
1 small onion
1 clove garlic
1 tsp tomato purée
1 tsp basil (fresh or dried)
1 tbsp olive oil
Salt and pepper
5 tbsp dairy-free margarine
3 tsp Worcestershire sauce
900g/2lb chicken breast
200g/7oz plain crisps

**Recipe Idea**
The tomato sauce can be served warm or cold, as it is or blended smooth using a hand blender.

1 Start with the sauce. Boil a kettle of water. Put tomatoes in a bowl and cover with boiling water. Leave for 1–2 minutes. Remove with a slotted spoon, slide skins off and discard. Chop flesh into small chunks.

2 Peel and chop onion, peel and crush clove of garlic. Heat olive oil in a saucepan and gently cook onion and garlic for 5 minutes with a lid on, but stir often.

3 Add chopped tomatoes, tomato purée, basil and salt and pepper. Stir well and cover pan with a lid. Simmer for 10 minutes. Remove lid, stir ingredients and leave uncovered to simmer for another 10 minutes.

4 Preheat the oven to 220°C/425°F/Gas 7. In a small saucepan melt the margarine and pour into a large bowl, add Worcestershire sauce. Cut chicken into 2.5cm/1in chunks. Add them to the margarine and stir well to coat in melted margarine.

5 Seal crisps in plastic bag and crush with a rolling pin. Use slotted spoon to add chicken pieces to the bag.

6 Shake well to coat evenly. Put chicken nuggets onto baking tray and bake for 10 minutes. Test a chicken nugget to make sure cooked through.

# Mini Pizzas

These pizzas are handy for a quick summer lunch in the garden, or for a children's tea. The uncooked dough can be made ahead and keeps in the freezer for up to 2 months.

## Ingredients for 4:

650g/1lb 7oz strong
   wholemeal flour
1 tsp salt
1x7g sachet easy-blend yeast
1 tsp soft dark brown sugar
2 tbsp vegetable oil
370ml/12fl oz lukewarm water

## Topping:

350g/12 jar chunky tomato
   pizza sauce
2 peppers, sliced
225g/8oz button
   mushrooms, sliced
275g/10oz mozzarella
   cheese, thinly sliced

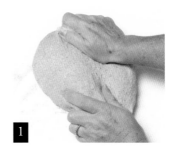

1 Mix the flour, salt, sugar and yeast powder together. Whisk the oil and water together and stir into the flour. Mix to a soft dough, turn on to a floured surface and knead for 10 minutes until smooth.

2 Return to the bowl. Cover with oiled clingfilm and leave until doubled in size, for about 30 minutes. Turn out and punch the air out of the dough. Cut into four (eight) equal pieces and roll each one into a ball.

3 Preheat the oven to 220°C/425°F/Gas 7. Grease two baking sheets. Roll each ball to a 12.5cm/5 inch circle and place on the baking sheets.

4 Spread each pizza base with 1½ (3) tablespoons of tomato sauce. Scatter the sliced peppers and the sliced mushrooms over the sauce, then top each with the sliced mozzarella cheese.

5 Leave for 15 minutes until the bases are puffy, then bake for 20 minutes until the bases are crisp and the topping golden and bubbling. Serve immediately.

# Cheesy Sausage Hot Dogs

A tasty fast-food for vegetarians anf non-vegetarians alike.

## Ingredients for 4

75g/3oz mature cheese
75g/3oz mushrooms
150g/5oz breadcrumbs
Salt and pepper
2 eggs
2 onions
50g/2oz butter
4 finger rolls
Tomato sauce

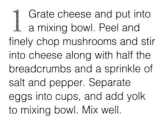

1 Grate cheese and put into a mixing bowl. Peel and finely chop mushrooms and stir into cheese along with half the breadcrumbs and a sprinkle of salt and pepper. Separate eggs into cups, and add yolk to mixing bowl. Mix well.

2 With wet hands, shape the mixture into eight sausages. Put egg white into one shallow dish and whisk lightly with a fork. In the other dish put remaining breadcrumbs.

3 Roll each sausage in egg white and then into breadcrumbs.

4 Preheat grill and cook sausages for 10–15 minutes, turning regularly.

5 Peel and slice the onions. Melt butter in a frying pan and then cook onion rings until soft and starting to brown.

6 When sausages and onions are cooked, slice down centre of each finger roll, put in a sausage (or two!), and top with cooked onion and tomato sauce.

# Thai Fish Cakes

You'll need a small food processor to make this dish. These machines are a great investment and save on time and washing-up.

## Ingredients for 2

50g/2oz fresh white bread, crusts removed
250g/9oz cod, skin and bones removed
½ chilli, deseeded and chopped
2.5cm/1in piece fresh root ginger, peeled and finely chopped
1 tbsp fresh coriander, chopped
2 tsp fish sauce
1 egg white
Salt
1 tbsp sunflower oil
Mixed salad leaves
Chilli dipping sauce

## Ingredients for 4

100g/4oz fresh white bread, crusts removed
500g/1lb 2oz cod, skin and bones removed
1 chilli, deseeded and chopped
5cm/2in piece fresh root ginger, peeled and finely chopped
2 tbsp fresh coriander, chopped
1 tbsp fish sauce
2 egg whites
Salt
2 tbsp sunflower oil
Mixed salad leaves
Chilli dipping sauce

1 Place the bread in a food processor and process into fine crumbs.

2 Chop the cod into chunks and remove any fine bones. Add the fish to the processor with the breadcrumbs, chilli, ginger, coriander, fish sauce and egg white. Season with a little salt.

3 Process the mixture until blended and smooth. Divide into 4 (8) pieces and shape into patties.

4 Heat the oil in a large non-stick frying pan and fry the cakes for 3 minutes on each side until golden brown. Pat with kitchen paper and serve with the salad leaves and dipping sauce.

# Fruit Fairy

If you like coconut, you'll love this! Coconuts are the largest "seeds' known to man, and every bit of the palm and fruit is used. This is a 'mocktail', but if you have a dash of crême de banane handy, then you can make a real cocktail!

## Ingredient for 1

1 small banana, peeled and chopped

25ml/1fl oz coconut cream

50ml/2fl oz pineapple juice, or 2 slices fruit, fresh or canned

2 scoops ready-made vanilla ice cream.

Put the banana and the pineapple (or juice) into the blender with the coconut cream and blend until smooth. Stop the blender and add the vanilla ice cream and blend again briefly. Pour into a glass and pop a cherry on top if you like.

# Chocolate Fondue

An easy and fun treat which is ideal for parties.

## Ingredients for 4-5

200g/7oz sweet good-quality
   chocolate
300ml/½ pt double cream
8 tbsp condensed milk
1 tsp vanilla extract

### Dippers
A selection of fruit
Marshmallows

1 Prepare the fruit that you
   want to use as dippers.
Wash fruit and remove stalks,
skin or stones. Chop into bite-
size pieces.

2 Arrange dippers onto large
   plate or platter.

3 If using bananas and
   apples give them a squirt
with lemon juice to prevent
them turning brown.

4 To make fondue, break
   chocolate into pieces and
put into a saucepan. Add
cream and condensed milk.
Melt over a low heat, stirring
occasionally until sauce is
smooth. Add vanilla extract and
stir again.

5 Pour sauce into a fondue
   pot or small bowls. Use
fondue forks or toothpicks to
'spear' the fruit and sweets. Dip
into chocolate and enjoy!

# Sprinkle Cake

An easy cake to make, and a colourful treat that children will love making – and eating!

## Ingredients

175g/6oz self-raising flour
1 tsp baking powder
175g/6oz margarine or butter
175g/6oz caster sugar
3 eggs
1 tsp vanilla essence
75g/3oz multi-coloured sprinkles

### Icing

175g/6oz butter/margarine
1 tbsp milk
175g/6oz icing sugar
1 tbsp cocoa powder
Extra multi-coloured sprinkles
6 glacé cherries

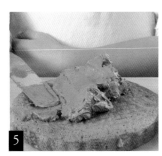

1 Preheat oven. Grease both sandwich tins and line the bases with greaseproof paper.

2 Sift flour and baking powder into a mixing bowl. Add butter/margarine, caster sugar, eggs and vanilla essence.

3 Combine the mixture using wooden spoon or hand whisk.

4 Add multi-coloured sprinkles and fold in with a metal mixing spoon.

5 divide mixture evenly between sandwich tins. Bake in oven for 20 minutes, and check to see if the cake is cooked. Leave to cool in the tins for 5 minutes then turn out onto a wire cooling rack. Leave to cool completely.

# Cinnamon Toasts

Serve this hot and tasty French toast for dessert or for a weekend brunch.

## Ingredients for 2

100g/4oz white, thick-sliced
  bread
1 egg, beaten
4 tbsp milk
½ tsp ground cinnamon
1 tbsp caster sugar
25g/1oz butter
2 tbsp golden syrup

## Ingredients for 4

200g/8oz white, thick-sliced
  bread
2 eggs, beaten
8 tbsp milk
1 tsp ground cinnamon
2 tbsp caster sugar
50g/2oz butter
4 tbsp golden syrup

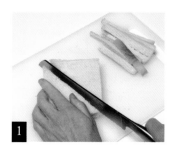

1 Cut the crusts from the bread, then cut the slices in half into triangles.

2 Beat the eggs, milk and half the cinnamon and sugar together. Quickly dip half the bread into the egg mixture to coat it. Melt half the butter in a large, non-stick frying pan.

3 Cook the slices in the butter for 2 minutes on each side until golden then keep warm. Melt the remaining butter, dip the remaining bread and cook as above.

4 Mix the remaining spice with the caster sugar and sprinkle over the toasts. Drizzle over the syrup and serve immediately.

# Straight from the Veg Patch

This takes planning and cooking a meal to a completely different level than just opening the fridge and store cupboard. The sense of achievement gained from growing your own food is fantastic and the end product often tastes a whole lot better than sore-bought. If you do not have the space for a vegetable patch so you could try growing salad and vegetables in pots, which is surprisingly easy. Each recipe focuses on one main ingredient. Whatever gem you take from your veg patch, this chapter will give you fresh cooking ideas for it!

# Sweet & Spiced Carrots

A simple dish that is a tasty accompaniment.

## Ingredients for 2

1 tbsp sunflower oil
2 shallots, peeled and
    chopped
1 clove garlic, peeled and
    finely chopped
1 tsp smoked paprika
350g/12oz carrots, peeled
    and sliced into batons
1 eating apple, cored and
    thinly sliced
100ml/3 ½fl oz apple juice

## Ingredients for 4

2 tbsp sunflower oil
4 shallots, peeled and
    chopped
2 cloves garlic, peeled and
    finely chopped
2 tsp smoked paprika
700g/1½ lb carrots, peeled
    and sliced into batons
1 large eating apple, cored
    and thinly sliced
200ml/7fl oz apple juice

1 In a large saucepan with a well-fitting lid, heat the oil over a moderate heat. Add the shallots and garlic and cook until softened.

2 Add the smoked paprika and cook for 1 minute, stirring. Stir in the carrots and apple, mixing well to coat in the shallots and spiced oil and cook for 2–3 minutes.

3 Pour over the apple juice and bring gently to the boil. Reduce the heat to a gentle simmer and cover the pan. Cook for 20 minutes until the carrots are tender. Serve.

# Smoked Sweet Potato & Chilli Soup

This is an easy-to-make soup that is just as good as a Saturday lunch after tearing around the supermarket as it is as a starter at a dinner party.

**Ingredients for 2**

1/2 tbsp oil
1 small onion, peeled and chopped
1 small clove garlic, peeled and crushed
¼ tsp dried red-chilli flakes
½ tbsp smoked paprika
250g/9oz sweet potatoes, peeled & cut into chunks
500ml/18fl oz vegetable stock
Salt and freshly ground black pepper
3 tbsp crème fraîche

**Ingredients for 4**

1 tbsp oil
1 onion, peeled and chopped
1 clove garlic, peeled and crushed
½ tsp dried red-chilli flakes
1 tbsp smoked paprika
500g/1lb 2oz sweet potatoes, peeled & cut into chunks
1l/1¾ pt vegetable stock
Salt and freshly ground black pepper
6 tbsp crème fraîche

1 In a large saucepan heat the oil over a moderate heat and cook the onion until it softens. Now add the garlic, chilli flakes and paprika and cook for 3 minutes, stirring well to mix.

2 Now add the sweet potatoes and toss well to coat in the spiced onion mixture. Cover with a lid, turn the heat to low and let the mixture cook for 5 minutes. Pour in the vegetable stock and increase the heat to bring up to boiling point. Stir well, then reduce the heat to simmering and cook covered for 20 minutes.

3 Remove the pan from the heat and allow to cool a little. Then purée the mixture with a hand blender or a food processor. Be very careful as sometimes hot liquids can splash out when processed.

4 Once smooth return the mixture to the pan and bring gently back to the boil. Season to taste and stir through the crème fraîche before serving.

# Cauliflower & Potato Curry

This dish is also known as aloo gobi and is a favourite in our family. I like to serve it with a dish of dhal, and some plain boiled rice. Garnish it with flaked or curled coconut, available from health food stores.

## Ingredients for 2

1 small cauliflower
2 tsp sunflower oil
2 tsp black mustard seeds
½ tsp ground turmeric
225g/8oz potatoes, peeled and cubed
50g/2oz frozen peas
1 chilli, deseeded and chopped
Small bunch fresh coriander, chopped
Coconut curls to serve

## Ingredients for 4

1 medium-sized cauliflower
1 tbsp sunflower oil
1 tbsp black mustard seeds
½ tsp ground turmeric
450g/1lb potatoes, peeled and cubed
100g/4oz frozen peas
2 chillies, deseeded and chopped
Large bunch fresh coriander, chopped
Coconut curls to serve

1 Break the cauliflower into florets and add to a large pan of boiling, salted water. Boil for 2 minutes then drain.

2 Heat the oil in a large pan or wok and add the mustard seeds and turmeric. Fry for 1 minute then add the potatoes and stir-fry for 1 minute to coat the cubes in the spices.

3 Add 150ml/¼pt (300ml/½pt) of water, stir and cover with a lid or piece of foil and cook for 10 minutes.

4 Add the peas, chillies and cauliflower, cover and cook for 10 minutes until the vegetables are soft and the liquid has reduced. Fold in the coriander and serve sprinkled with coconut curls.

# Penne with Broccoli

You'll only need one pan to prepare and cook this quick amd easy supper.

| Ingredients for 2 | Ingredients for 4 |
|---|---|
| 175g/6oz broccoli florets | 450g/1lb broccoli florets |
| 200g/7oz penne pasta | 350g/12oz penne pasta |
| 100g/4oz sun-dried tomatoes in oil | 200g/7oz sun-dried tomatoes in oil |
| 1 tbsp olive oil | 2 tbsp olive oil |
| 75g/3oz goat's cheese | 175g/6oz goat's cheese |
| Black pepper, freshly ground | Black pepper, freshly ground |

1 Bring a large pan of salted water to the boil and cook the broccoli florets for 4 minutes until tender.

2 Lift the broccoli from the pan with a slotted spoon and drain in a colander. Add the pasta to the same water in the pan and cook, according to the pack instructions until al dente. Drain well.

3 Return the pasta and broccoli to the pan. Drain the sun-dried tomatoes, chop coarsely and add to the pan.

4 Toss together with the olive oil and divide between warmed serving bowls. Crumble over the goat's cheese and serve immediately, seasoned with freshly ground black pepper.

# Herb Omelette

If you wish to make one large omelette, use a big frying pan and slice the omelette after cooking. If you prefer, vegetarian Parmesan is now widely available from supermarkets and specialist shops.

## Ingredients for 2

4 eggs
2 tbsp parsley chopped
1 tbsp chives chopped
butter for greasing
15g/½ oz Parmesan, finely
    grated
Salt and freshly ground
    black pepper to taste

## Ingredients for 4

8 eggs
4 tbsp parsley chopped
2 tbsp chives chopped
butter for greasing
25g/1oz Parmesan, finely
    grated
Salt and freshly ground
    black pepper to taste

1 Separate the eggs and beat the yolks together with a little salt and pepper. Now, using a whisk, whip the egg whites until they reach soft-peak stage.

2 Using a large metal spoon, gently fold the egg whites and chopped herbs into the egg yolks. Preheat the grill to high.

3 Lightly grease a small frying pan with a little butter and place over a moderate heat. Add half (a quarter) of the egg mixture and cook for 2–3 minutes. Scatter over half (a quarter) of the Parmesan, then place the pan under the preheated grill. Cook for 1 minute until golden in places and springy to the touch. Remove from the heat and serve. Repeat with the remaining mixture.

# Warm Tomato & Green Bean Salad

By cooking the tomatoes in this way the flavour becomes much more intense.

| Ingredients for 2 | Ingredients for 4 |
|---|---|
| 250g/9oz cherry tomatoes, halved | 500g/1lb 2oz cherry tomatoes, halved |
| 225g/8oz fine green beans, trimmed | 450g/1lb fine green beans, trimmed |
| 1 tbsp balsamic vinegar | 2 tbsp balsamic vinegar |
| 1 tbsp olive oil | 2 tbsp olive oil |
| 1 tbsp basil leaves shredded | 2 tbsp basil leaves shredded |
| Freshly ground black pepper | Freshly ground black pepper |

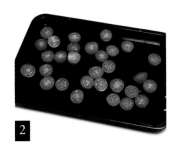

1 Preheat the oven to 130°C/250°F/Gas ½. Line a heavy-gauge baking tray with silicone sheet or baking parchment or alternatively use a non-stick one.

2 Arrange the tomatoes in a single layer over the prepared baking sheet and cook in the preheated oven for 2½–3 hours until the tomatoes are semi dried.

3 About ten minutes before the tomatoes are ready, bring a large saucepan of water to the boil and then cook the beans for 3–4 minutes until just tender but still with a little bite. Drain.

4 Toss the beans, balsamic vinegar and oil through the semi-dried tomatoes and return to the oven for 5 minutes. Sprinkle with shredded basil leaves, season with freshly ground black pepper and serve.

# Stuffed Aubergines

Although aubergines are now available all year round, they are generally cheaper during the summer, making this an economical, as well as a delicious, warm-weather dish.

## Ingredients for 2

1 large aubergine
salt
2 tbsp olive oil
1 onion, peeled and chopped
1 small clove garlic, peeled and crushed
1 celery stalk
2 large tomatoes, peeled and chopped
½ tbsp tomato purée
¼ tsp allspice
1 tbsp fresh parsley, chopped
25g/1oz pitted black olives
freshly ground black pepper
½ tsp sugar
½ lemon, juiced
75g/3oz mozzarella, drained and sliced
Basil for garnishing

## Ingredients for 4

2 large aubergines
salt
4 tbsp olive oil
1 large onion, peeled and chopped
1 clove garlic, peeled and crushed
2 celery stalks
4 large tomatoes, peeled and chopped
1 tbsp tomato purée
½ tsp allspice
3 tbsp fresh parsley, chopped
50g/2oz pitted black olives
freshly ground black pepper
1 tsp sugar
1 lemon, juiced
150g/5oz mozzarella, drained and sliced
Basil for garnishing

1. Preheat the oven to 180°C/350°F/Gas 4. Cut the stalks off the aubergines and then slice in half lengthways. Using a spoon scoop out as much of the flesh as possible leaving approximately 1cm/½in thickness all round.

2

7

2 Roughly chop the flesh and reserve. Sprinkle the insides of the aubergine skins liberally with salt and place them cut side down on a plate for about 30 minutes.

3 Heat 3–4 tbsp of the oil in a large frying pan and cook the onions over a moderate heat for 5 minutes until softened. Add the garlic and celery and cook for a further 3–4 minutes.

4 Stir in the tomatoes and chopped aubergine flesh and cook for 10 minutes to soften.

5 Add the tomato purée, allspice, parsley and olives. Season to taste. Remove from the heat.

6 Rinse the aubergine skins thoroughly and pat dry with kitchen paper. Place in a shallow ovenproof dish. Divide the mixture between the aubergine skins.

7 Mix the lemon juice and sugar with 150ml/¼pt (300ml/½pt) boiling water and the remaining oil and pour around the aubergines, being careful not to pour it into the aubergines. Cover loosely with tinfoil, pinching round the edges to seal. Bake in the preheated oven for 45 minutes. Remove the foil and top each aubergine with the mozzarella slices. Return to the oven for a further 15 minutes. Serve garnished with basil.

# Spinach & Goat's Cheese Pizza

Making your own pizza dough produces a very crisp base, and really isn't that difficult.

## Serves 12

125g/5oz white-bread flour
1 pinch sugar
¼ tsp salt
½ tsp dried, easy-action yeast
1 tbsp olive oil
50g/2oz spinach
50g/2oz cherry tomatoes
50g/2oz goat's cheese
Coarse cornmeal or polenta
Salt and freshly ground
    black pepper

## Serves 24

250g/9oz white-bread flour
¼ tsp sugar
½ tsp salt
1 tsp dried, easy-action yeast
2 tbsp olive oil
100g/4oz spinach
100g/4oz cherry tomatoes
100g/4oz goat's cheese
Coarse cornmeal or polenta
Salt and freshly ground
    black pepper

1 Sift the flour into a mixing bowl. Add the sugar and salt and stir to mix. Sprinkle over the yeast and mix.

2 Stir half of the olive oil into 75ml/5 tbsp (150ml/¼pt) tepid water. Make a hollow in the flour and pour in the water and oil mix, drawing the flour in from the sides to make a smooth dough. Turn out onto a lightly floured surface and knead for 10 minutes until the dough is smooth and springy to the touch. Return to the mixing bowl and cover with clingfilm. Leave in a warm place for 1–2 hours or until the dough has doubled in size.

3

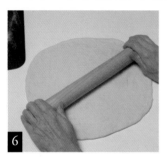

6

3 Meanwhile wash the spinach and shake to remove as much of the water as possible. Roughly shred using a large sharp knife. Place in a saucepan and heat, stirring, until it just starts to wilt. Drain thoroughly and set to one side.

4 Halve the cherry tomatoes and thinly slice the goat's cheese.

5 When the dough is puffy and double in size, preheat the oven to 240°C/475°F/Gas 9. Lightly oil a baking sheet and sprinkle with the cornmeal.

6 Remove the dough from the bowl and knead briefly on a floured surface. Now roll and stretch into a large round 35cm/14in. Place on the prepared baking sheet.

7 Sprinkle over the prepared spinach and tomatoes. Drizzle over the remaining olive oil. Top with the slices of goat's cheese and bake in the preheated oven for 8–10 minutes. Serve.

# Creamy Courgette Tart

Some supermarkets sell ready-made pastry cases, and if you are in a hurry, you could use one of these instead of the shortcrust pastry specified in the list of ingredients.

## Ingredients for 4-6

400g/14oz shortcrust pastry
450g/1lb courgettes
150g/5oz soft garlic-and-herb cheese
1 egg
Salt and freshly ground black pepper

1 On a lightly floured surface roll out the pastry and use to line a 23cm/9in shallow, loose-bottomed tart tin. Trim the excess pastry with a small, sharp knife. Chill the pastry for 30 minutes. Preheat the oven to 200°C/400°F/Gas 6 and place a baking sheet in the oven to heat.

2 Line the pastry case with a piece of greaseproof paper and then fill with baking beans. Bake the pastry case on the preheated baking sheet for 10 minutes. Remove the greaseproof paper and the baking beans and return the pastry case to the oven for a further 5 minutes. Set to one side while you make the filling.

3 Wash and trim the courgettes. Coarsely grate into a bowl.

4 In a small bowl beat the cheese a little to loosen. In a small bowl beat the egg and then add a little at a time to the cheese, beating well between each addition.

5 Mix the cheese mixture into the courgettes. Season with salt and pepper. Fill the pastry case with this mixture, levelling a little with the back of a spoon.

6 Place in the oven on the baking sheet and cook for 30 minutes, or until set. Remove and allow to cool for 10 minutes before serving.

# Leek & Cheese Soufflés

These soufflés should be served straight from the oven, while they're golden and risen.

## Ingredients for 2

Butter for greasing
15g/½oz Parmesan cheese,
   finely grated
½ tbsp sunflower oil
1½ large leeks, washed and
   finely sliced
1 small clove garlic, peeled
   and crushed
3 eggs
2 tbsp single cream
25g/1oz wholemeal
   breadcrumbs
50g/2oz Cheddar cheese,
   grated
½ tsp dried mixed herbs
Salt and freshly ground
   black pepper

## Ingredients for 4

Butter for greasing
25g/1oz Parmesan cheese,
   finely grated
1 tbsp sunflower oil
3 large leeks, washed and
   finely sliced
1 clove garlic, peeled and
   crushed
6 eggs
4 tbsp single cream
50g/2oz wholemeal
   breadcrumbs
100g/4oz Cheddar cheese,
   grated
1 tsp mixed herbs
Salt and freshly ground
   black pepper

1 Preheat the oven to 200°C/400°F/Gas 6. Lightly grease 2 (4) ovenproof 450ml/¾pt bowls. Coat with the Parmesan, reserving any that does not stick to the sides. Set to one side.

2 Heat the oil in a large frying pan and cook the leeks and garlic for 10 minutes until softened. Leave to cool a little.

3 Separate the eggs. Add the cream, breadcrumbs, Cheddar, mixed herbs and any remaining Parmesan to the egg yolks and beat.

4 Stir in the cooked leeks and beat again. Season with salt and freshly ground black pepper.

5 Whisk the egg whites until they form soft peaks. Using a large metal spoon gently fold the egg whites through the leek mixture.

6 Divide the mixture between the prepared bowls. Bake in the preheated oven for 15–20 minutes until golden and springy to the touch. Serve.

# Particularly Delicious

Some recipes seem quite ordinary when you first look at them. The ingredients may not be anything special, perhaps, or the recipe simply looks too straightforward to be anything out of the ordinary. In this way, some of the most delicious recipes are often overlooked. This chapter contains 10 such recipes – simple and unassuming, but very, very tasty!

# Butter Bean Stew

This is a quick version of a bean dish eaten in Greece during the Lenten months before Easter.

## Ingredients for 2

1 tbsp olive oil
1 shallot, chopped
1 stick celery, sliced
1 clove garlic, peeled and
   chopped
200g/7oz can chopped
   tomatoes
¼tsp paprika
125ml/4fl oz vegetable stock
400g/14oz can butter beans
1 sprig fresh oregano or 1
   tsp dried oregano
Salt
Black pepper, freshly ground
1 tbsp fresh flat leaf parsley,
   chopped

## Ingredients for 4

2 tbsp olive oil
2 shallots, chopped
2 sticks celery, sliced
2 cloves garlic, peeled and
   chopped
400g/14oz can chopped
   tomatoes
½tsp paprika
250ml/8fl oz vegetable stock
2 x 400g/14oz cans butter
   beans
1 sprig fresh oregano or 1
   tsp dried oregano
Salt
Black pepper, freshly ground
2 tbsp fresh flat leaf
   parsley, chopped

1 Heat the oil in a large frying pan and fry the shallots, celery and garlic for 3 minutes to soften.

2 Add the tomatoes, paprika and stock to the pan and stir together. Drain and rinse the beans under cold running water.

3 Add the beans to the pan with the oregano and season with salt and freshly ground black pepper.

4 Simmer, covered, for 15 minutes until the mixture thickens. Sprinkle with chopped parsley and serve with crusty bread.

# Layered Root Loaf

This savoury loaf is a good source of vitamin C, E, folate and fibre.

## Ingredients for 4-6

Oil for spraying
400g/14oz potatoes, peeled
400g/14oz parsnips, peeled
400g/14oz sweet potato, peeled
1 egg
1 clove garlic, finely chopped
1 tbsp fresh chives, chopped
1 tbsp fresh parsley, chopped
150ml/¼pt vegetable stock
Salt and freshly ground black pepper to taste

1  Lightly oil and base-line a 23 x 12.5 x 7.5cm (9 x 5 x 3in) loaf tin. Preheat the oven to 190°C/375°F/Gas 5. Slice all the vegetables as thinly as possible. This is best done on a mandolin or in a food processor with a thin cutting disc. If using a sharp knife, try to get them all a similar thickness.

2  In a jug, beat the egg together with the garlic and chopped herbs. Add the vegetable stock and mix again. Place a single layer of the potatoes in the bottom of the prepared tin. Top these with a layer of the parsnips followed by a layer of the sweet potato. Continue in this way, repeating the layers and seasoning lightly every few layers, until all the vegetables have been used up.

3  Pour the egg and stock mixture evenly over the layered vegetables. It is best to do this slowly so the liquid has time to soak down through the layers.

4  Cover with foil, pinching around the edges to seal.

5  Bake in the preheated oven for 1½ hours. Remove the foil and return to the oven for a further 30–40 minutes. Test with a knife to check the loaf is tender and cooked through. Turn out onto a plate and serve cut in slices.

# Beetroot Risotto

Parmesan is a high-fat cheese but it is so rich in flavour that a little goes a long way. It is a good source of calcium, which is essential in a healthy diet.

## Ingredients for 2

225g/8oz ready-cooked
   beetroot
2 tsp olive oil
15g/½oz butter
1 red onion, peeled and
   finely chopped
500ml/18fl oz vegetable
   stock
150g/5oz brown rice
15g/½oz Parmesan shavings
Salt and freshly ground black
   pepper to taste

## Ingredients for 4

450g/1lb ready-cooked
   beetroot
4 tsp olive oil
25g/1oz butter
1 large red onion, peeled and
   finely chopped
1 l/1¾pt vegetable stock
300g/10½oz brown rice
25g/1oz Parmesan shavings
Salt and freshly ground black
   pepper to taste

1 Cut the beetroot into small dice and set to one side. Heat the oil and butter in a large saucepan over a moderate heat. Add the red onion and cook over a moderate heat until it is transparent and softened.

2 Place the stock in a saucepan, bring to the boil, then reduce the heat to a very gentle simmer. Cover. Add the rice and stir well to coat in the mixture. Cook for 1–2 minutes. Add three to four ladles of the hot stock to the rice mixture, stirring well to mix. Cook, stirring gently, until the liquid has almost been absorbed before adding another three to four ladles of the hot stock.

3 When almost half the stock has been added, stir in the beetroot. Continue adding the stock until the rice is tender and most of the liquid has been absorbed. You may not need all the hot stock, just keep adding it until the risotto is to your liking. Sprinkle with the Parmesan, season and serve.

# Tomato & Sardine Pasta

Sardines provide us with omega-3 fatty acids.

## Ingredients for 2

1 tbsp olive oil
1 onion, peeled and finely
    chopped
2 cloves garlic, peeled and
    finely chopped
4 sun-dried tomatoes
1 x 200g/7oz can tomatoes,
    chopped
200g/7oz mafalde pasta
1 tsp red wine vinegar
1 x 120g/4½oz can sardines
3 tbsp fresh basil

## Ingredients for 4

2 tbsp olive oil
1 large onion, peeled and
    finely chopped
4 cloves garlic, peeled and
    finely chopped
8 sun-dried tomatoes
1 x 400g/14oz can tomatoes,
    chopped
400g/14oz mafalde pasta
2 tsp red wine vinegar
2 x 120g/4½oz cans
    sardines
6 tbsp fresh basil

1 Heat the oil in a frying pan over a moderate heat and cook the onion until softened. Add the garlic and cook for 2–3 minutes until softened but not browned.

2 Roughly chop the sun-dried tomatoes and add to the pan, stirring well to mix.

3 Stir in the chopped tomatoes and cook at a gentle simmer until thickened.

4 Meanwhile bring a large saucepan of water to the boil and cook the pasta according to the packet instructions. Drain.

5 Add the vinegar and sardines to the frying pan and cook, stirring, for 2–3 minutes until piping hot. Serve spooned over the pasta and sprinkled with the shredded basil.

# Frying Pan Pizza

You won't need to turn your oven on to make this tasty pizza – add all your favourite toppings, plus plenty of melted cheese.

## Ingredients for 2

150g/5oz packet pizza-base mix
2 tbsp sunflower oil
1 large onion, sliced into rings
100g/4oz mushrooms, sliced
100g/4oz tomato passata
1 tsp dried oregano
1 tbsp capers in brine, drained
75g/3oz salami slices, halved
6 anchovies in oil, drained and halved
100g/4oz mozzarella cheese, chopped

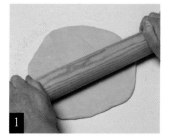

1 Make the pizza base up with water following the pack instructions, knead well and roll out to a circle large enough to fit inside a 25cm/10in frying pan.

2 Heat 1 tablespoon of the oil and cook the onions and mushrooms for 5 minutes until soft. Remove from the pan with a slotted spoon.

3 Heat the remaining oil and place the dough in the pan. Cook over a medium heat for 5 minutes until the base is lightly browned. Turn the base over and cook for a further 5 minutes.

4 While the other side is cooking, spoon over the passata and herbs. Arrange the cooked onions and mushrooms, then top with the capers, salami, anchovies and cheese. To serve, place the pan under a hot grill and grill for 2 minutes until the cheese is bubbling. Lift out of the pan with two spatulas and cut into four wedges to serve.

# Bacon & Bean Minestrone

You can make this warming soup ahead of time, as the flavours improve on reheating, or make a double batch for the freezer.

## Ingredients for 2

2 tsp olive oil
1 small onion, peeled and chopped
50g/2oz streaky bacon, rinds removed and diced
1 clove garlic, peeled and crushed
1 stick celery, finely chopped
1 large carrot, diced
2 tbsp tomato purée
600ml/1pt vegetable stock
400g/14oz can cannellini beans, rinsed and drained
½ small savoy cabbage, finely shredded
Salt
Black pepper, freshly ground

## Ingredients for 4

1 tbsp olive oil
1 large onion, peeled and chopped
100g/4oz streaky bacon, rinds removed and diced
2 cloves garlic, peeled and crushed
2 sticks celery, finely chopped
2 carrots, diced
4 tbsp tomato purée
1l/1¾pt vegetable stock
2 x 400g/14oz cans cannellini beans, rinsed and drained
1 small savoy cabbage, finely shredded
Salt
Black pepper, freshly ground

1 Heat the oil in a large pan and fry the onion and bacon until golden, for about 2 minutes.

2 Add the garlic, celery and carrot and fry for 4 minutes then stir in the tomato purée and the stock. Bring to the boil, then cover and simmer for 10 minutes.

3 Add the beans and the cabbage and simmer for a further 10 minutes until the cabbage is tender.

4 Taste the soup and season then serve in warmed bowls with chunks of crusty bread.

# Bubble & Squeak

Great for using leftover potato or cabbage, but delicious enough to make from scratch. Although bubble and squeak can be used as a side dish I think it makes a great midweek meal in itself, especially if served with bacon and grilled tomatoes.

## Ingredients for 2

500g/1lb 2oz floury potatoes, peeled
100-175g/4-6oz cabbage or spring greens
25g/1oz butter
1 tbsp sunflower oil
Salt and freshly ground black pepper

## Ingredients for 4

900g/2lb floury potatoes, peeled
225g/8oz cabbage or spring greens
40g/1½oz butter
2 tbsp sunflower oil
Salt and freshly ground black pepper

1 Cut the potatoes into large dice.

2 Bring a pan of lightly salted water to the boil. Add the potatoes and return to the boil. Simmer for 5–8 minutes until tender.

3 Drain and mash well.

4 Meanwhile, shred the cabbage and cook in another pan of boiling water for 4–5 minutes until tender. Drain well.

5 Heat the butter and oil in a heavy-based frying pan.

Add the potato and cabbage and mix together. Season with salt and pepper.

6 Spread out in a layer in the pan and cook for 2–3 minutes until a crust forms on the base.

7 Break up the mixture, then press down into the pan and cook for a further 1–2 minutes.

8 Repeat this once or twice more so that the bubble and squeak is piping hot and there are bits of golden, crispy potato crust in the mixture. Serve immediately.

# Carob Cake

One of our friends can't eat chocolate as it gives her headaches, so I make this cake using carob which tastes just as chocolately. You'll find it on sale in health-food shops.

## Ingredients

2 tbsp carob powder
225g/8oz soft-tub margarine
225g/8oz soft dark brown
   sugar
4 eggs
1 tsp vanilla essence
225g/8oz self-raising flour

## Filling

425g/15oz can crushed
   pineapple
225g/8oz full-fat cream
   cheese
1 tbsp caster sugar
225g/8oz fromage frais
75g/3oz carob bar

1 Preheat the oven to 180°C/35°F/Gas 4. Grease and line the bases of two 20cm/8in round sandwich tins. Mix the carob powder to a paste with 4 tbsp of cold water.

2 Place all the remaining cake ingredients into a large bowl and add the carob paste. Beat together for about 2 minutes until light and fluffy. Spread into the tins and make a slight hollow in the centres.

3 Bake for 30-35 minutes until springy in the centres. Cool in the tins for 10 minutes, then cool on a rack.

4 To make the filling, drain the pineapple in a sieve and chop finely if there are any large pieces. Soften the cream cheese in a bowl, fold in the fromage frais and the sugar, then stir in the pineapple.

5 Sandwich the cake together with one-third of the filling, then spread the remainder over the top and sides. Grate the carob bar into large flakes and sprinkle over the cake.

# Rhubarb & Orange Pots

Fresh rhubarb is delicious combined with orange in these creamy little desserts.

**1**

## Ingredients for 2

225g/8oz fresh, pink rhubarb,
    chopped
25g/1oz butter
Finely grated zest and juice
    of ½ orange, plus some
    thin strips of zest
25g/1oz caster sugar
150ml/¼pt double cream

## Ingredients for 4

450g/1lb fresh, pink rhubarb,
    chopped
50g/2oz butter
Finely grated zest and juice
    of 1 orange, plus some
    thin strips of zest
50g/2oz caster sugar
300ml/½pt double cream

**2**

1 Place the rhubarb in a pan
   with the butter, orange rind
and juice and 1 (2) tbsp of
water.

2 Cover and simmer gently
   for 8 minutes until the
rhubarb is soft. Stir in the sugar
and taste the fruit, if it is too
sharp, add more sugar. Place
in a bowl to cool.

3 Whip the cream until thick
   and fold into the cold fruit.
Spoon into 2 (4) small serving
dishes or glasses and chill for
20 minutes.

4 Just before serving,
   sprinkle with thin strips of
orange zest.

**3**

## Cook's Tip

If you don't have rhubarb to hand, you could use 450g/1lb fresh,
ripe gooseberries instead.

# Creamy Pan-cooked Macaroni Pudding

When I was a child, Sunday lunch was often followed by a baked macaroni pudding. This is a quicker stove-cooked version of a childhood favourite.

## Ingredients for 2

75g/3oz short-cut macaroni
1 tablespoon golden syrup
200g/7oz can evaporated milk
Ground nutmeg or cinnamon to sprinkle

## Ingredients for 4

150g/6oz short-cut macaroni
2 tablespoons golden syrup
400g/14oz can evaporated milk
Ground nutmeg or cinnamon to sprinkle

1 Cook the pasta in plenty of boiling water for 8–10 minutes or until only just tender.

2 Drain and return to the pan.

3 Stir in the golden syrup and evaporated milk.

4 Simmer gently for 5–10 minutes until creamy, then pour into a serving dish and sprinkle with nutmeg or cinnamon.

# Yummy Treats

It's easy to make a favourite dish so often that it loses it's "treat-value". So the following recipes aren't for everyday consumption - they need to be saved and made on very special occasions (well that's the sensible idea). They include a range of savoury and sweet treats equally good for any occasion from children's parties to accompanying barbeques or to go with grown up drinks.

# Corn Fritters

Children love these crisp, golden fritters. Serve them piping hot with a vegetable or salad of your choice. They also taste good when teamed with a chilli dipping sauce.

**Ingredients for 2**

½ egg, beaten
½ tbsp Thai green-curry paste
125g/5oz sweet corn, canned
    or frozen
3 spring onions
½ tbsp mint
2 tbsp coriander
25g/1oz plain flour
Salt and freshly ground
    black pepper
Oil for shallow-frying
Lime wedges & salad to serve

**Ingredients for 4**

1 egg, beaten
1 tbsp Thai green-curry paste
250g/9oz sweet corn, canned
    or frozen
6 spring onions
1 tbsp mint
4 tbsp coriander
50g/2oz plain flour
Salt and freshly ground
    black pepper
Oil for shallow-frying
Lime wedges & salad to
serve

1 In a large mixing bowl beat the egg together with the curry paste. Stir in the sweetcorn kernels.

2 Trim and finely slice the spring onions and add to the beaten egg. Remove the coarse stems from the mint and discard. Finely chop the coriander and mint.

3 Stir the chopped herbs through the sweetcorn mixture. Sprinkle over the flour and mix. Season lightly with salt and freshly ground black pepper.

4 Heat the oil in a frying pan over a moderately high heat. Cook spoonfuls of the mixture until golden, then turn and cook the other side.

5 Drain on kitchen paper and keep warm while you cook the remaining mixture.

6 Serve with lime wedges and salad.

# Mixed Potato Crisps

The hand-fried crisps available in the shops taste great but are expensive. Why not make your own? If you have a deep-fat fryer it's very easy. I like to use a mixture of regular and sweet potatoes; occasionally I also fry slices of parsnip, beetroot and carrot.

Ingredients for 2

200g/7oz potatoes
100g/4oz sweet potatoes
oil for deep-frying
¼ tsp dried thyme
sea salt, preferably Maldon
freshly ground black pepper

Ingredients for 4

400g/14oz potatoes
200g/7oz sweet potatoes
oil for deep-frying
½ tsp dried thyme
sea salt, preferably Maldon
freshly ground black pepper

1 Peel the potatoes and cut into very thin slices with a sharp knife, a mandolin or in a food processor.

2 Heat the oil for deep-frying to 190°C/375°F.

3 Deep-fry the potato slices in batches for 2–3 minutes until crisp and golden.

4 Remove the basket from the oil and shake off any excess oil. Tip the crisps onto a tray lined with kitchen paper.

5 Serve sprinkled with dried thyme, salt and pepper.

# Cheese & Walnut Straws

Ingredients for 2

**Ingredients for 2**

50g/2oz plain flour
40g/1½oz butter, chilled
25g/1oz mature Cheddar
    cheese
15g/½ oz Parmesan cheese
1 pinch cayenne pepper
40g/1½oz walnut pieces
1 beaten egg for brushing over
Salt and freshly ground
    black pepper

**Ingredients for 4**

100g/4oz plain flour
75g/3oz butter, chilled
50g/2oz mature Cheddar
    cheese
25g/1oz Parmesan cheese
¼ tsp cayenne pepper
75g/3oz walnut pieces
1 beaten egg for brushing over
Salt and freshly ground
    black pepper

Nobody can resist freshly baked cheese straws. Although I have provided quantities for two people, restrict yourself to these, and you'll probably wish that you'd made more!

1 Sift the flour into a bowl and, working quickly coarsely grate the butter into the flour. You will need to keep dipping the butter into the flour and sprinkling flour over the grater, to stop the butter from sticking but the end result is worth it.

2 Stir the mixture quickly with a knife to incorporate the butter through the flour. Place in the freezer to chill while you make the filling.

3 Coarsely grate the Cheddar cheese into a bowl. Finely grate the Parmesan and add it to the bowl along with the cayenne pepper. Coarsely chop the walnuts and add to the cheese mixture.

4 Preheat the oven to 220°C/425°F/Gas 7. Remove the bowl from the freezer and add enough cold water to make a firm dough. Add the water a little at a time: if you add too much water it will make the pastry tough. Stir the water in with a knife, until it looks like you have almost added enough. Now use your fingertips and bring it quickly together.

5 On a lightly floured surface roll out the pastry to a thickness of 5mm/¼in using a rolling pin. Brush the surface with a thin coating of the beaten egg. Now sprinkle a third of the cheese mixture over half of the pastry. Fold the uncovered piece of pastry over the cheese and nuts, pressing down well with the rolling pin to seal.

6 Give the pastry a quarter turn. Roll out again to 5mm/¼in and repeat the whole procedure. Now brush the top of the pastry lightly with the egg and sprinkle over the remaining cheese and walnuts, pressing down to seal. Cut into thin strips and place on a baking sheet, allowing room between each one to rise. Bake in the oven for 10–12 minutes. Cool on a wire rack and serve.

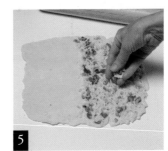

# Fruity Punch

This is a lovely drink for a summer's day in the garden.

4 oranges
½ lemon
½ lime
1 apple
2 tbsp sugar
8 cocktail cherries
500ml/18fl oz apple juice
500ml/18fl oz pineapple juice
1l/1¾ pt lemonade

1 Squeeze orange juice and add to large jug or bowl. Cut lemon and lime into slices and add to jug.

2 Cut apple into quarters and remove core. Slice apple.

3 Add to jug. Stir in sugar and cocktail cherries. Pour in fruit juices and lemonade. Stir well and serve.

# Knickerbocker Glory

This must be one of the best-known and most-loved puddings in the world!

## Ingredients for 2

300ml/½pt set strawberry jelly (make the day before)
2 small scoops of strawberry ice cream
2 small scoops vanilla ice cream
1 bananas
1 kiwis
125g/4oz strawberries
2 wafers
½ can ready-whipped cream
Sugar sprinkles to decorate

### For sauce

75g/3oz strawberries
75ml/2 fl oz double cream
1 tsp caster sugar

## Ingredients for 4

600ml/1pt set strawberry jelly (make the day before)
4 small scoops of strawberry ice cream
4 small scoops vanilla ice cream
2 bananas
2 kiwis
225g/8oz strawberries
4 wafers
1 can ready-whipped cream
Sugar sprinkles to decorate

### For sauce

175g/6oz strawberries
150ml/¼pt double cream
2 tsp caster sugar

1 Place sauce ingredients in a bowl and, using hand blender, blend until everything is mixed together.

2 Wipe strawberries and remove the stalks, then slice. Peel kiwi fruit and slice, peel bananas and also slice.

3 In each tall glass, spoon a layer of jelly and add a scoop of vanilla ice cream.

4 Divide fruit between glasses and drizzle two tablespoons of strawberry sauce into each glass.

5 Add a thin layer of jelly followed by a scoop of strawberry ice cream. Top with more strawberry sauce and a wafer. Squirt whipped cream on top and decorate with sugar sprinkles. Serve with a long-handled spoon.

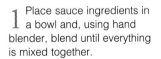

# Chocolate Cookies

For chocolate-lovers everywhere.

Ingredients for 12 cookies

80g/3oz dark chocolate
25g/1oz butter
25g/1oz plain flour
Pinch of baking powder
1 egg
125g/4oz caster sugar
50g/2oz small chocolate chunks

1 Preheat the oven to 180°C/350°F/Gas 4. Line a baking tray with a piece of greaseproof paper.

2 To make the cookies, break the dark chocolate into pieces and place in a heatproof bowl, along with the butter. Melt over a pan of simmering water, stirring. When melted, remove from the heat and allow to cool slightly.

3 In a bowl, beat the egg and sugar until pale and thick. Stir in the melted chocolate, then sift in the flour and baking powder and stir well. Finally add the chocolate chunks and stir until well combined.

4 Using a tablespoon, drop one spoon per cookie onto the prepared baking tray. Bake for 8–10 minutes. Then transfer to a wire rack to cool.

# Millionaire's Shortbread

You'll always be popular with your guests when you serve these chocolate-topped, luxury layers.

## Ingredients for 9 squares

100g/4oz butter, softened
50g/2oz golden caster sugar
175g/6oz plain flour

## Topping

175g/6oz plain chocolate,
  broken into squares

## Caramel

400g/14oz can condensed
  milk
2 tbsp golden syrup
100g/4oz golden caster
  sugar
100g/4oz butter

1 Preheat the oven to 180°C/350°F/Gas 4. Grease and line the base of a 20cm/8in square tin with non-stick baking paper.

2 Beat the butter and sugar together until pale and fluffy. Mix in the flour and knead in the bowl until smooth.

3 Press the mixture into the tin and prick the surface with a fork. Bake for 20–25 minutes until light golden. Cool in the tin on a wire rack.

4 To make the caramel layer, put the condensed milk, syrup, sugar and butter in a heavy-based saucepan. Heat gently until every grain of sugar has dissolved.

5 Bring to the boil and boil for 6–8 minutes, stirring continuously, until light golden and thickened. Pour the caramel over the biscuit base to cover it completely. Leave until cold and set.

6 Melt the chocolate in a bowl standing over a pan of warm water, or alternatively, in the microwave on Low. Spread over the caramel with a palette knife and leave to cool and set. Mark into 9 squares to serve.

# Fruit Pavlova

The perfect pudding for a summer meal. It is important to make sure you really whisk the egg-white well, otherwise your meringue will be floppy!

*Ingredients for 6 people*

3 egg whites
Pinch of salt
250g/9oz caster sugar
1 tsp vanilla essence
1 tsp white vinegar
300ml/10fl oz fresh double cream
700g/1½ lb fresh fruit e.g.
    strawberries, raspberries, kiwi
    fruit, grapes

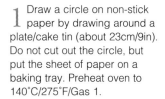

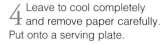

1 Draw a circle on non-stick paper by drawing around a plate/cake tin (about 23cm/9in). Do not cut out the circle, but put the sheet of paper on a baking tray. Preheat oven to 140°C/275°F/Gas 1.

2 Put egg whites and salt into a mixing bowl and whisk until very stiff. Sift quarter of the sugar into bowl and whisk. Add another quarter and whisk again. Repeat until all sugar has been added. Beat until mixture forms stiff peaks when whisk is removed.

3 Add vanilla essence and vinegar, and whisk until mixed in. Use a palette knife to spread mixture over paper circle, and bake in oven for 1 hour until firm.

4 Leave to cool completely and remove paper carefully. Put onto a serving plate.

5 In a clean bowl, whisk double cream until stiff and put on top of meringue leaving a 1 cm (½ in) gap around the edges. Prepare the fruit by washing it and removing any skin or stalks. Put fruit on top of cream and meringue.

# Banana Splits with Chocolate Sauce

Get the kids involved and let them help create these special treats.

1 Break the chocolate into squares and place in a heatproof or microwave-proof bowl with the butter and syrup. Heat over a pan of simmering water or in the microwave on Low until melted.

2 Peel the bananas and cut them in half lengthways. Whip the cream until it forms soft peaks then fold in the icing sugar and the vanilla extract.

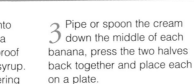

3 Pipe or spoon the cream down the middle of each banana, press the two halves back together and place each on a plate.

4 Spoon a tablespoon of toffee sauce over each banana then drizzle each one with chocolate sauce. Sprinkle with nuts and serve immediately.

# White Chocolate Gateau

This delicate gateau is smothered in a delightful white chocolate cream. It is delicious served with fresh strawberries or raspberries in the summer.

## Ingredients for 8

50g/2oz white chocolate
175g/6oz butter or block
    margarine
175g/6oz caster sugar
3 eggs, beaten
175g/6oz self-raising flour
Finely grated zest of ½ a
    lemon

## Filling and Topping

150ml/¼ pt whipping cream
3 tbsp chocolate nut spread
225g/8oz white chocolate
200ml/7fl oz crème fraîche

1 Preheat the oven to 180°C/350°F/Gas 4. Grease and line the bases of two 19cm/7½ in sandwich tins with non-stick baking paper. Grate the white chocolate finely.

2 Place the butter and sugar in a bowl and beat with an electric mixer until soft and fluffy. Gradually add the eggs, using a little flour with each addition. Fold in the flour, zest and grated chocolate.

3 Spoon into the tins and spread level. Bake for 20–25 minutes until golden and just firm to the touch. Turn out to cool on a wire rack.

4 For the filling, whip the whipping cream until stiff, then divide in half. Mix half with the chocolate nut spread and use to sandwich the cakes together.

5 For the topping, break the white chocolate into pieces and melt in the microwave on Low. Alternatively, melt in a bowl set over a pan of warm water. Beat together with the crème fraîche and cool for 5 minutes. When cold, fold in the whipped cream and spread over the top and sides of the cake.

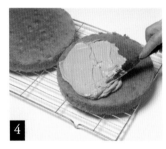

# index

ale 89
almonds 57
anchovies 186
apples 71, 127, 155, 213
  juice 155, 213
apricot 75
aubergine 39, 169

Baba Ghanoush 39
bacon 188
Bacon & Bean Minestrone 190
banana 144, 201, 217
Banana Splits with Chocolate
Sauce 219
basil 41, 44, 136, 165, 185
bay leaves 93
Bean Burgers 121
beans 51, 117, 119, 165, 179
beef 23, 47, 93, 109, 137
Beef Pot-roast 47
beetroot 182
Beetroot Risotto 184
biscuits 31, 35, 52, 133, 204
BLB Cupcakes 104
bread 41, 143, 150
breadcrumbs 24, 119, 135, 140
broccoli 87, 163
brown ale 89
brown rice 129, 182
Bubble & Squeak 193
butter beans 179
Butter Bean Stew 181

cabbage 188, 191
  red 71
cakes 33, 57, 75, 101, 102,
149, 192, 218

cannellini beans 51, 119, 188
capers 186
carob 192
Carob Cake 194
Carrot & Pea Flan 21
carrots 21, 27, 43, 60, 73, 87,
107, 155, 188
cauliflower 87, 159
Cauliflower & Potato Curry 161
cayenne pepper 207
celery 73, 89, 167, 179, 188
Cheddar cheese 97, 109, 175,
207
cheese 16, 35, 41, 65, 75, 82,
85, 87, 97, 109, 114, 117, 135,
139, 140, 161, 163, 167, 169,
175, 182, 186, 207
Cheese & Walnut Straws 207
cheesecake 35
Cheesy Sausage Hot Dogs 142
cherries 35, 55
  cocktail 213
  glacé 75, 149
Cherry Cheesecake Slices 35
Cherry Clafouti 55
Cheshire cheese 82
chicken 24, 62, 68, 107, 136
Chicken Goujons 24
Chicken Nuggets with Tomato
Sauce 138
Chicken Spiced Rice 109
chick-peas 71, 94
Chick-peas & Potatoes 96
chilli 23, 27, 39, 94, 107, 119,
143, 156, 159
  sauce 27, 143
Chinese leaf 43
chives 82, 163, 181

chocolate 52, 75, 78, 146, 204,
211, 217, 218
Chocolate Bread & Butter
Pudding 80
Chocolate Cookies 212
Chocolate Fondue 148
cinnamon 125, 150, 197
Cinnamon Toasts 152
cocoa 52, 77, 149
coconut 144, 159
cod 143
coffee 52
cookies, see biscuits
coriander 23, 27, 39, 94, 98,
107, 119, 143, 159, 202
Coriander & Lentil Soup 100
Corn Fritters 202
courgette 85, 107, 117, 173
cream 19, 78, 146, 175, 195,
201, 214, 217
cream cheese 35, 65
Creamy Courgette Tart 175
Creamy Mushroom & Ham
Bake 65
Creamy Pan-cooked Macaroni
Pudding 199
Creamy Tomato & Thyme
Shells 116
crème fraîche 48, 68, 125, 156
Crispy Potato Balls with Chilli
Dip 27
croissants, chocolate 78
cucumber 19
cumin 23, 39, 94, 119

digestive biscuits 35
duck 43
Duck & Honey Stir-fry 43

Dundee Cake 57

fennel 94
feta cheese 16
fish 19, 85, 112, 143, 185, 186
fish cakes 143
fish sauce 143
fondue, chocolate 148
Frittata 119
fritters 202
fruit, dried 57, 75
Fruit Fairy 146
Fruit Pavlova 216
Fruity Punch 209
Frying Pan Pizza 188

garlic 21, 23, 39, 41, 47, 67, 68, 71, 89, 98, 107, 109, 114, 119, 135, 136, 155, 156, 167, 175, 179, 181, 185, 188
ginger 94, 98, 107, 143
goat's cheese 161, 169
Goulash 51
Granny Smith Sorbet 129
green beans 117, 167

ham 65
Herb Omelette 165
Highland Fling 124
Home-made Lemonade 28
honey 43

ice cream 144, 201

jelly 201

kiwi fruit 201

Knickerbocker Glory 211

lamb 60,62
Lamb Hotpot 60
lavender 31
Lavender Cookies 31
Layered Root Loaf 183
Leek & Cheese Soufflés 177
leeks 175
lemon 19, 28, 33, 35, 39, 44, 57, 94, 122, 167, 213, 218
lemonade 28, 213
Lemon Cupcakes 33
lentils 73, 98
lime 213

marshmallows 146
mascarpone cheese 77
Meadow Pie 73
meatballs 135
Millionaire's Shortbread 215
mincemeat 77
Mincemeat Cake 77
Mini Pizzas 141
mint 202
Mixed Potato Crisps 204
mozzarella cheese 41, 139, 167, 186
Mozzarella & Peppers in a Crusty Roll 41
Mushroom & Ale Pie 91
mushrooms 65, 91, 93, 139, 140, 186

olives 117, 167
omelette 163
onion 16, 21, 23, 43, 47, 51, 62, 65, 68, 71, 73, 85, 89, 93, 94, 98, 107, 109, 112, 117, 119, 135, 136, 140, 155, 156, 167, 179, 182, 185, 186, 188, 202
orange 125, 133, 195, 213
oregano 135, 179, 186

Oven-baked Tuna Risotto 87

pancetta 135
paprika 41, 51, 68, 107, 155, 156, 179
Parmesan cheese 85, 117, 135, 163, 175, 182, 207
parsley 21, 44, 48, 85, 89, 163, 167, 179, 181
parsnips 60, 181
pasta 19, 97, 114, 135, 161, 185
pastry 23, 89, 173

pavlova 216
pears 127
peas 21, 27, 87, 159
Penne with Broccoli 163
peppers 16, 41, 51, 107, 112, 117, 139
pesto 67
pies 16, 73, 87, 89
pineapple 144
  juice 213
Pinwheel Cookies 52
pizza 139, 169, 186
pork 48
Pork Tenderloin Roast 48
Potato & Chicken Goulash 68
Potato Moussaka 111
potatoes 16, 23, 27, 51, 60, 62, 65, 67, 68, 73, 82, 84, 94, 111, 112, 117, 159, 181, 191, 208
  sweet 47, 156, 181, 208
pot-roast 47, 62, 95
Pot-roast Brisket 95
Pot-roast Chicken 62
pudding rice 129
pumpkin 87
prunes 75, 129

raspberries 124
Red Cabbage & Chick-pea Bake 71
red Leicester cheese 87
red kidney beans 119
rhubarb 197
Rhubarb & Orange Pots 197
rice 107
  brown 129, 182
  pudding 129

risotto 85
ricotta cheese 114
risotto 85, 182
rosemary 48
Rustic Pie 16

sage 97
salads 19, 165
salami 186
salmon 44
  smoked 19
Salmon Steaks with Lemon Butter 44
sardines 185
Sausage, Tomato & Pasta Supper 99
sausages 67, 97
Savoury Potato Scones with Cheese & Chives 84
savoy cabbage 188
scones 82
shallots 47, 93, 135, 155, 179
Sizzling Sausage Bake 67
Smoked Salmon & Cucumber Pasta Salad 19
Smoked Sweet Potato & Chilli Soup 158
sorbet 127
soup 98, 156, 188
soured cream 19
soy sauce 43, 107
Spaghetti & Meatballs 137
Spiced Poached Pears 127
Spicy Beef & Potato Crescents 23
spinach 171
Spinach and Goat's Cheese Pizza 171

spring onions 43, 202
Sprinkle Cake 151
star anise 125
stir-fry 43
strawberries 79, 201
Strawberries with Mascarpone 79
Stuffed Aubergines 169
Sultana Cookies 135
Sweet & Spiced Carrots 157
sweetcorn 87, 202
sweet potato 47, 156, 181, 208
Swiss Roll 103

tahini 39
Thai Fish Cakes 145
thyme 71, 73, 93, 114, 208
Tomato & Sardine Pasta 186
tomatoes 67, 73, 85, 94, 99, 114, 135, 136, 139, 161, 165, 167, 169, 179, 185, 186
tuna 85, 114
turmeric 23, 94, 159

vanilla 31, 35, 52, 55, 78, 125, 131, 146, 149, 192, 214, 217
Vanilla Rice Pudding 131
Vegetable Potato Pie 89

walnuts 75, 207
Warm Tomato & Green Bean Salad 167
Warm Tuna & Roasted Pepper Salad 114
White Chocolate Gateau 220
Worcestershire sauce 136

yoghurt 94